WHAT PEOPLE ARE
"What's Going o

This little volume will revolutionize your life as you witness the vibrant account of God's work among the Bisorio people in distant Papua New Guinea.

"What's Going on Downriver?" brings you into a remote village held in the bondage of Satanic spiritism. You experience the challenge of capturing a primitive language, the rigors of Bible translation, and the amazing story of how "God's Talk" touches lives.

Take the trip "downriver" and you will be lifted right into God's presence.

DR. J. RONALD BLUE
International Mobilizer of Latin Missions, CAM_International
Coordinator – Spanish Doctor of Ministries
Dallas Theological Seminary

This was an "I can't put it down book" for me! *What's Going on Downriver* is an inspiring account of God's love reaching out to sinners. This is a riveting, real life account of a lost world turned upside down by the love of God in modern times.

This true story has been captured in a compelling way that will stir the missionary mandate God has placed in the heart of every believer.

This narrative provides valuable insights to understanding how any culture void of the truth about God can effectively be penetrated – allowing God's timeless truth be told.

What's Going on Downriver will serve the cause of the Gospel well. It is a simple but profoundly powerful account of real life missions work.

Dr. Bob Smith
Senior Pastor, Mt. Spokane Church
Chaplain, Spokane Fire Department

This is a book that every missions-minded person will want to complete in one sitting.

Can the concepts of God, the Creator and God, the Deliverer from sin, self and Satan, be conveyed to the Bisorio people of Papua New Guinea? Rob Greenslade, a seasoned pastor, relates to us how this Himalayan task was wrought by the Holy Spirit through the labors of the missionaries of New Tribes Mission.

D. John Richard,
Minister-at-Large, ACTION International Ministries

This is what Christianity is all about...ordinary people doing extraordinary things for God! Two American families; the Kennells and the Walkers, "White Skins," with the common goal of bringing "God's Talk" to the Bisorio people.

Establishing trust, struggling to learn an unknown and unwritten language, overcoming cultural barriers, myths, and, of course, the tribal witch doctor are just a few of the daunting challenges these families faced.

All these challenges are captured in this gripping true story. "What's Going on Downriver?" is an exciting narrative that captivates you from page one and keeps you riveted until the end.

This story was so moving that it caused me to reflect on my relationship with Jesus, and to remember that God is truly able to do immeasurably more than we can ask or imagine.

-Kari Udlock

This is a wonderful example of God in action building His church, through four frail, fearful but faithful vessels. They dared to believe and trust God in the face of spiritual hopelessness and darkness.

As I read this book my eyes and heart welled up with tears of joy. I witnessed the love of God soften the hearts of the Bisorios. I felt the struggle of learning an unwritten language. I sensed light dispelling the darkness as the Gospel was shared clearly. I saw the convicting work of the Holy Spirit as the Bisorios agreed with God concerning their sin. I was reminded again of the life, death, burial and resurrection of God's dear Son, Jesus. Thank You Lord!

I cheered as the Bisorios began to understand the love, mercy and grace of God. I was awed at the power of God to forgive, cleanse, adopt and indwell the Bisorios. He gave everlasting life to a people who, in the past, had no hope.

Paul C. Dye
New Tribes Mission Aviation

Rob Greenslade is a skilled observer and writer, with an insider's knowledge of tribal missions and church planting. This story of a missionary family in Papua New Guinea and their adventure in connecting to their tribe and breaking through the translation barriers will connect with anyone who has ever dreamed of the exotic world of jungles and dug-out canoes and drums in the night.

On a technical level, Greenslade interacts with issues of folk religion and syncretism in a very readable way. His portrayal of the practice of tribal linguistics is both accurate and touching.

"What's Going On Downriver" is a quick and enjoyable read for anyone with a love for God's Word and the adventure of tribal missions, and will serve admirably as an introduction to the field. I will recommend this book to my students.

Dr John McMath
Professor of Bible – Moody Bible Institute—Spokane

"What's Going On Downriver?"
Isolated, fearful…a forgotten people

by

Rob Greenslade

Dedication

This book is lovingly dedicated to

George and Harriett Walker

and

Bob and Noby Kennell

who have given their lives to bring
"God's Talk" to the Bisorio people of
Papua New Guinea.

Table of Contents

Preface to

What's Going On Downriver?

This true story is groundbreaking, because it tells of one of the first church planting efforts in modern times where the missionaries employed "chronological" Bible teaching.

While most Americans have at least a small degree of Bible knowledge, many nations (people groups), have absolutely no background of biblical truth. The chronological method of Bible instruction recognizes that the people being taught have no previous Bible knowledge. Thus, the attitude and approach of the missionaries is, "start from the beginning!" The beginning of the Bible is the Old Testament, starting with the book of Genesis. The Old Testament is truly the foundation for Christianity. Thus, before a person is introduced to God as his Savior, he must first understand that God is his Creator. Before he realizes he is a sinner, a man must see that God is Holy. All these foundational truths are found in the Old Testament. (See appendix A for more on chronological Bible teaching)

Although the Bible teaching given to the Bisorio people was taught chronologically, we have chosen to tell their story in a different way! The reader will be introduced to them at a time when the missionaries have already lived with them for about six months. The time is February 1979. The place is Papua New Guinea....

(1)

The Rage of Kabalame

(February, 1979 Papua New Guinea)

His jealousy and anger exploded into rage; "If I kill you now," he screamed, "It'll be *your* fault, not mine!" Whirling away from his hysterical wife, he grabbed his 8-foot hunting spear. But she was young and quick. As soon as he turned for the spear, she bolted out the door of their hut.

Wild-eyed with anger, Kabalame burst out the door after her, screaming for her to come back. But she fled down the path on the west side of the village, wailing frantically. He sprang after her like a hunter pursuing his quarry, with his spear ready to run her through.

"Gai mimidobaba! (You're a harlot, aren't you!) He yelled as he gave chase. But his wife, Doneyaka had a good lead – terror gave wings to her bare feet! And now, the whole village was in an uproar, as the terrified wailing of the woman and the furious ravings of the man shattered the usual morning sounds.

15

They pelted down the path toward the river, their dark skin glistening with sweat and their vine skirts flapping behind them. Instinctively, she darted from side to side to avoid being impaled. Kabalame, nearly blind with fury, closed the gap between them. At the bottom of the village, she turned and sprinted up the path past the missionary's house. Her enraged husband slowed for a second when he heard one voice above the confusion…

"Wao, Kabalame! Ade biyoino! ("No, Kabalame! Don't do this!") He recognized the voice: It was the meddling, white-skin, yelling out his window. Kabalame felt a fleeting twinge of guilt, but his jealousy kept him on the chase. After flying past the missionary's house, he was suddenly grappled from behind and his arms were pinned to his sides. As he stumbled to a halt, he heard the white-skin's voice right in his ear; "Wao, Kabalame! Ade biyoino!"

Kabalame grimaced and looked down; the white arms wrapped around him and the clasped white hands moved with his heaving chest. Then he looked up as Doneyaka scampered back up the hill to their thatched hut. A wave of shame and embarrassment swept over him, momentarily subduing his rage. He felt the arms around him relax.

George Walker loosened his grip. It had all happened so incredibly quickly, he hadn't had time to think. Six months of living with the Bisorio people had taught him that wife beating was not uncommon; but wife killing? What was he supposed to do…be "culturally sensitive," and let Kabalame spear his wife? No, he had to do something! So he threw caution to the wind, and flew out of his house just in time

to grab Kabalame! Now, as he released the breath-
less Bisorio man, George wondered if *he* would be
speared instead of Doneyaka! As the angry husband
turned to face the missionary, George was relieved
to see other men from the village trotting over. He
didn't yet understand enough of their language to
probe into Kabalame and Doneyaka's domestic
war, but, thankfully, Hadebaiyo was coming over.
He spoke "Pidgin English," the common trade language of Papua New Guinea and would be able to
interpret for the missionary.

Kabalame was still volatile. When the other
men arrived, he began shaking his spear, gesturing
wildly toward his hut and yammering in his own
language.

"What is he saying?" George asked Hadebaiyo
in Pidgin. Hadebaiyo interpreted and the story
began to unfold:

Two days earlier, some young men from another
village had passed through and stayed for a short
time in Kabalame and Doneyaka's hut. During their
visit, Kabalame saw his wife and one of the young
men making eye contact. There is a particular eye
signal and eye response in their culture that means,
"I want you," and "I accept." This jealous husband
thought that he had seen his young wife "making
eyes" with the guest.

Kabalame had seethed and simmered for two
days, and finally he had confronted his wife. In the
Bisorio language, adultery is called, "stolen intercourse." He angrily accused his bride of planning
to commit "stolen intercourse" with the young man.

Doneyaka immediately denied it. But, he was insistent; he *knew* what he saw! When she continued to deny it, he slapped her and told her to confess. She screamed her denial back at him. Anger boiled over in both of them as accusations and curses flew from one to the other. That was when he had grabbed his spear...

As he heard the story, George knew that Kabalame felt completely justified in wanting to spear his wife. Adultery was often punishable by death, and in this culture a woman had little right to defend herself. But even though Kabalame felt that his anger was legitimate, he was known throughout the tribe as having a violent temper. Americans might call him a "loose cannon." In their tongue, Kabalame was called, "one whose anger is always near!" Usually, though, after his emotional "explosions," he calmed down and became rational. So, George hoped that with the help of the Bisorio men he would cool down. They talked together for ten to fifteen minutes, letting his rage subside. Finally, Kabalame slung his spear over his shoulder and trudged up the hill toward his hut...just past the home of George's co-workers, the Kennells.

George watched with a heavy heart as the Bisorio man headed home. He was reasonably sure that Doneyaka would not be speared to death...at least, not today. But knowing Kabalame's violent temper, most likely more beatings and retaliation would follow. George knew he would have to explain the whole crazy affair to the other missionaries. It was so difficult to have to endure the domestic squabbles that rocked the village nearly every day. It was hard enough to stay focused on the disciplines of learning this unknown, unwritten language. But these huge distractions always took a toll on their progress in language learning.

He took a deep breath and sighed. The pungent citrus smell of the jungle grasses filled his senses. Then he gazed at the sun, its brightness softened by the mists of morning. There was incredible beauty and wonder surrounding this remote village in the land of Papua New Guinea. But there was no beauty in what he had just witnessed between Kabalame and Doneyaka. He thought sadly of their little daughter, the precious two year old who shared the hut with them; what about *her* future? Would she, one day, be married to a wife beater? George grieved over the bleak prospects for the women in this culture.

Then he reflected upon why he and his family had come to this forgotten corner of the world: "We've got the life-changing message," he thought. "We have the Good News that can transform Kabalame's life!" But the Bisorio language was unwritten and completely unknown to the outside world. He and his co-workers had at least two, and possibly three more years before they grasped the language and culture well enough to share the message.

George shook his head and muttered, "I wonder if I will *ever* be able to communicate with them?" He sighed again and walked into his house to get his pen and note pad. He did not have time to grieve over the insanity of what had happened; he had to attend to the business at hand…another day in the village, mingling with the Bisorio people to try to learn a little more of their language.

(2)

The Invitation

(Now we must "rewind the tape" to February
of 1978 to discover what brought two
families all the way from America to move
into this tiny village in Papua New Guinea.)

From within the mosquito netting surrounding their two sleeping bags, the American "white skins" witnessed an eerie show! The light from the setting sun revealed hundreds of huge, malaria-laden mosquitoes flitting and dancing, seeking entrance into their sleeping space!

"Have you ever seen so many mosquitoes?" Steve asked, as he tried to slide down deeper into his bag.

"We've got to look on the bright side;" replied Bob, "At least they're friendly!"

* * * * * * * * * * * * * * *

The basin of the Sepik River in Papua New Guinea doesn't attract many visitors. The climate is attractive only to "trophy" mosquitoes! The daily temperature is 110 degrees, with a "cool" 85 at night! The humidity always hovers at about 100 percent. And, there is virtually no breeze to bring relief.

But Bob Kennell and Steve Lawrence were not on "holiday." They were making their way up the Yokopas River to try to make contact with a tribe of people called the "Bisorios." They had made this same trip before and found only a deserted village. They later learned that a terrible epidemic had struck the area and had forced the Bisorios to flee from their most dreaded evil spirit, Gonimai, who they believed was the malicious power behind the sickness.

Now, four months later, Bob and Steve again steered their small motorboat toward this tiny Bisorio community called Basababi. They started their journey at the town of Amvunti, an established missions station about 30 miles east of their destination. It took them full two days to make the trip, traveling on three rivers; the Sepik, the Crossameri and finally, the Yokopas.

As they cut through the steamy, oppressive air brooding over the river, the white skins were drenched in sweat. The river wound its way through virgin jungle, and the gigantic trees lining the banks watched silently as these foreigners plowed through the silty water. Where the river narrowed, the treetops formed a canopy and threw tangles of jungle vines down to the water, as if to forbid the intruders from passing any further.

But the missionaries pressed on, and when they finally glided to the bank at Basababi, they knew that the plague had passed, for they were greeted by the thirty Bisorios who were now living there. The arrival of these two "hone" (white skins) was a big event, and as Bob and Steve stepped out of the boat the people crowded around these tall foreigners, curious as to their intentions. But only two of the Bisorio men could speak Pidgin English, the trade language, so communication was difficult.

Through halting words in Pidgin and lots of hand gestures, Bob tried to tell them that he and his family wanted to move into their village, tell them about God and give them "God's Talk." The men shrugged their shoulders and replied, "What is God?" After an hour of limited communication and "sign language," one of the men said (in so many words!),

"We must bring our "big" leaders here to talk. They will tell you if you can live with us, or not!" So, several of the Bisorios headed further upstream to find their headmen.

After these messengers took off hiking upriver, Bob and Steve evoked lots of interest from the villagers by communicating that the little white "eggs" in a bottle helped to get rid of headaches.

When it dawned on the Bisorios what they were saying, there was a sudden "epidemic" of headaches! Aspirin was entirely new to them!

It had been two hours since the missionaries had watched the messengers hike upstream. Suddenly, spine-chilling war whoops echoed and re-echoed down the little river! Riveted to their spot on the riverbank, Bob and Steve strained their eyes upriver. After a moment of tense waiting, two dugout canoes rounded the bend and came into view.

There were three men per craft. Their dark hair was plastered high on their heads, and little sticks poked out of their hair in all directions! They wore only grass "skirts" held together by jungle vines. Their chests were smeared with red and blue paint, and their nostrils were flared by bamboo "ornaments!" They clutched long spears and tall bows and arrows. As they drew closer, their faces looked stern, even angry. They were more wild and dangerous looking than anyone the missionaries had ever seen in Papua New Guinea!

Standing on the bank, wide-eyed as they approached, Bob Kennell found himself praying: "Father ... are You _sure_ you want me to bring my wife and two little kids in here to live with *these* guys?" He had left a comfortable life in America and come thousands of miles in hopes of bringing the Good News to a people who had never heard it. But now, the sight of these threatening looking warriors filled him with fear and doubt.

Yet, deep in his heart, he was sure of God's answer: There are only about 400 Bisorio people, but they have as much right as anyone to hear the Word of God! And *someone* has to take the step to bring the Word to them. So, this meeting with the Bisorio leaders was critical: Would these Bisorio warriors send them away at arrow-point, or would they ease up, and welcome his family into their village?

As the canoes drew nearer, the man in the lead boat held up his hand in token of peace and called out a greeting in the trade language. Bob heaved a sigh of relief. At least they weren't fitting arrows to their strings! Finally, here were the "big leaders;" men with whom he could communicate and get an answer to his request.

The spokesman for these Bisorio leaders was a man in his mid twenties named Hadebaiyo. All the other men jumped out of the canoes, but he remained with one foot on the bank and one in the canoe. The missionaries had no idea what to expect from them, but, to their complete surprise, as soon as Hadebaiyo dispensed with greetings, he began to describe the "badness" of his existence. He looked down and pointed to his sides—they were laced with long scars; it looked like he had been flogged with a whip around his pelvis and kidneys.

"Do you see these scars?" He said in the trade language. "They come from the jungle vines we use for our covering…they cut our flesh." he then pointed to his vine loincloth, "Would you be happy to wear this?" Before the missionaries could answer, he waved his hand toward the jungle:

"We live like animals, scratching out our living day to day. Wild pigs tear up our gardens. Our heads are crawling with lice, and the jungle is crawling with enemies from another tribe seeking to kill us! And if they can't spear us to death, they try to curse us through their witch doctor."

He became more animated as he spoke. "Our lives are very bad! We are miserable! Even with our witch doctor's help, we still suffer sickness. And there is one enemy that no shaman can defeat... Death! We live in constant fear of death. The messengers say you want to live with us...you want to help us...you want to give us God's talk. Do you really want to help us? If you do, then you are welcome here. Yes, come live with us!" The other leaders clicked their tongues in agreement. "Yes, and bring your families," they said earnestly.

Bob smiled and nodded his head in amazement. His Heavenly Father had immediately answered his prayer, and He couldn't have spoken any clearer: "Yes, Bob! I *am* sure that I want you and your family to move here!"

After all the months of praying and seeking, Bob Kennell was finally talking to the Bisorio leaders. And here they were, welcoming the missionaries with open arms!

* * * * * * * * * * *

And so it was that the village of Basababi became the home for Bob Kennell and his family. In March of 1978, their little house was started, just 100 yards up from the river bank where he had first met the Bisorio leaders. Their home was larger than a Bisorio hut, but constructed of the same materials: Large poles formed the foundation and main "skeleton" for the house; the walls were made of the fronds of sago palm trees; and the floors were made of tree bark. The roof was two-thirds thatch, and one third corrugated aluminum, used for collecting rainwater. (A metal roof was entirely impractical for the Bisorios, since they had no chimneys for their fireplaces and needed a thatched roof to allow the smoke to gather in the ceiling and then filter right through the thatch!)

After a couple of months of very hard work, Bob and his co-worker, assisted by many of the Bisorios, completed their little house overlooking the Yokopas river. In May of 1978, Bob was joined by his wife, Noby and their two little daughters, Karrie and Kristie.

In September of the same year, George and Harriett Walker and their infant son, Georgie were welcomed to "Bisorio Land!" They moved in with the Kennells. Then, thanks to the diligence of a support worker named Jack Housley, a second small "bush house" was finished for Walkers. These two young American families, the Kennells and the Walkers, became co-workers and friends with the common goal of bringing "God's Talk" to the Bisorio people.

The Bisorios are a semi-nomadic tribe and don't usually cluster together. They generally live in extended family units of two or three huts, which they relocate every few years. These tiny communities are called "hamlets," and are often a full day's hike from one another! But, as the first months came and went, more and more of the Bisorios built their huts in Basababi and "moved in!" So, the community on the Yokapas River slowly grew. Then, one word at a time, and one tradition at a time, the Kennells and Walkers began to learn the language and customs of the Bisorio people.

* * * * * * * * * * * * * * * *

The arrival of these two white families was, naturally, the hot topic of discussion among the tribe. The missionaries were very different in dress, culture, and language. They had incredibly pale skin and seemed to have no knowledge of how to survive in the jungle! But, they did have good medicine and were very willing to share it when the Bisorios or their children got sick. And, for some reason, the "hone" (white skins) were fascinated with the Bisorio language! Still, after several months, their presence was shrouded in mystery. Who were they? What were they...?

...Hadebaiyo listened to Kabalame and shook his head violently,

"Na sogowasedobaba?!" – "How am I supposed to know?" He answered. "Do you think *I'm* a dweller with the white men? I don't know what they *really* want! They say they want to give us 'God's Talk'... whatever that is! And then, they ask again and again, 'What is this?' So, I tell them for the 20th time, 'It's a tree!' They are incredibly slow learners!"

"But what is this 'God's Talk?'" Kabalame persisted. "If they want to give it to us, why don't they just *give* it to us and leave us alone?"

"They say they can only give it to us in our tongue," replied Hadebaiyo. "I tell them to say it in Pidgin, but they refuse! They are not only slow-minded, they're stubborn!"

"I wonder if they are even human," mused Kabalame. "Look at their skin; so sickly and pale! Could they be 'Sowanaga'... spirits of our dead ancestors? That's what many of our people fear. And that's why they refuse to come from our forefathers' ground and move down to this place."

"I'm sure they're human." Hadebaiyo smiled. "Haven't we seen them come down with malaria? And if they can get sick, they also can die!" He ran his thumb across the razor edge of his new machete. "I've seen them slice their fingers. I've seen their blood…it looks just like ours! O, yes, they are mortals, even as we are."

"And they seem to want to help us." he continued thoughtfully. "They have powerful medicine. They put the needle in our arm and the festering sores on our bodies just disappear! Even our Shaman can't do that! And look at this bush knife they gave me. It is so much better than the stone tools of our ancestors. Maybe, if we treat them well, they will give us better clothes to wear. I think we should watch and wait. Eventually, they will learn our language and then we'll see what this new message is all about."

"But the shaman has sent word from his hamlet that they might anger the spirits," Kabalame said, "If they are bringing a strange god here, Bagowai says a curse will come upon our gardens."

Hadebaiyo looked at his friend with a touch of compassion. "Kabalame, you're not afraid, are you? Listen, right now we have nothing to fear from these hone. They are stitching up our wounds. They are fixing our broken bones. They are giving us better tools. And, don't forget, we *invited* them to live with us, so our custom requires us to be kind to them. They have come from their ground, far away, downriver. So let's keep our eyes open and try to be as friendly to them as we can."

For a moment, the two Bisorio men were silent. Then, Hadebaiyo said in a lower voice,

"I was speaking truth to the white skins six moons ago when they first came. I told them that my life is miserable, and it is. I am *not* happy on the trail I'm walking. If they can show me a better path, I just might follow it!" (Appendix B)

(3)

<u>Just the Right Word</u>

(Spring, 1980)

Hadebaiyo was right; the white-skins were incredibly slow learners! But, the process of grasping an unknown and unwritten language is extremely tough!

The missionaries had no "English-Bisorio" dictionary! They not only had to hear and pronounce words and phrases that were entirely foreign, but they had to produce a phonetic alphabet and write everything down! It was all brand new. They were thankful for the training in language study they had received through New Tribes Mission. But since Bisorio is unlike any other language in the world, the process was slow and painstaking. Some of it was flat impossible....How in the world how do you write the phonetics of a war howl?

To add to the missionaries' difficulties, the Bisorios seemed to take fiendish delight in making fun of the "hone's slow tongues!" Bisorio culture embraces a wide range of sarcasm; their remarks, facial expressions, and gestures are often punctuated with ridicule. As they got to know the Walkers and Kennells, these masters of derision showed no mercy to the missionaries and their stumbling language learning! If a white skin couldn't make a certain sound in the Bisorio language, one of the villagers would try to get his hands in the missionary's mouth to adjust his tongue!

One of the most exasperating language setbacks for the missionaries was when a mischievous Bisorio "language helper" would actually substitute an *obscenity* in the Bisorio tongue, just for the fun of hearing the white skins say it! The unsuspecting missionary would use the dirty word while the villagers would do their best to hide their hilarity! Thus, language acquisition was very frustrating, time-consuming, and wearying.

Nevertheless, the missionaries made progress. They spent time among the villagers, learning the "every day" language of the home, the garden and the hunt. And, as they got to know the people, Bob and George picked out men who seemed to have a special aptitude for helping with language and took them into their grass hut "offices" for consultation on the Bisorio tongue. They sometimes spent hours with these language helpers trying to find certain Bisorio words that don't arise in common, day to day talk. These "one on one" times were very important because the Americans were preparing for the day they would teach the Word of God to the Bisorios, and there are key, biblical concepts that needed to be expressed in the language of the people.

Probably the most central concept to the message of Christ is expressed by our English word, "forgiveness." For, if our fellowship with God is blocked by sin, then that fellowship can only be restored through *forgiveness* of sin. After a year and a half with the Bisorios, Bob and George began a campaign to discover the Bisorio word for "forgiveness." But, two solid weeks of working with their language helpers brought them up empty-handed.

"Maybe there is no such word." Bob suggested as he and George chatted one morning.

"Well, this whole culture seems to revolve around justice," answered George, "Just look at their 'court system!' (Appendix C) They take one another to court for nearly everything! So perhaps there is no such thing as forgiveness; only strict justice, an 'eye for an eye' mentality."

"But, after a debt is paid, there must be a way to the Bisorio mind of expressing freedom from the debt." said Bob.

"You would sure think so; but I'm beginning to wonder," replied George.

Bob shook his head in frustration; "It's sure going to be tough to tell the Bisorios about God's wonderful forgiveness if they don't even have a similar word or phrase!"

"Well my brother," said George, "I guess we're just going to have to pray and ask God to show us the Bisorio word for 'forgiveness.'"

Bob smiled and looked at his co-worker, "Pray, huh? Has it really come to *that?*"

So, as was their habit, these two men took this question to the Lord. And, as was *His* habit, He answered their prayer!

It happened a couple of days later as George, who was by now much more fluent in Bisorio, chatted with his language helper, Mawiba. They were together in the tiny building behind the Walker's house that served as the office, when Mawiba began describing an incident from the day before: He and one of his friends had been horsing around when, accidentally, his buddy had broken Mawiba's spear. So Mawiba had told him, "Nama halodaga sogao."

George put down his cup of coffee and grabbed his pen and notepad. "What was that you said to him?" he asked his friend.

"I said, 'Nama halodaga sogao.' ('I pluck off, and throw it away.')" answered Mawiba.

George wrote down the Bisorio phrase. "But what does that mean when you say it?"

"It means that, even though he broke my spear, I pluck off any concerns about it, and throw them away." said Mawiba.

"But he *still* broke your spear," queried George, "And therefore, he should repay you. It would be the *just* thing to do."

"Yes," responded Mawiba, "But since I told him that I pluck it off and throw it away, any concerns are 'dead;' never to be mentioned again."

"So, he doesn't have to pay you anything for the broken spear?"

"No, of course not. You don't pay for concerns that are dead."

"So, when you tell someone, 'nama halodaga sogao,' they never have to fear that the offense will be brought up again. The bad thing is forgotten?"

"That's right," answered Mawiba, "It has been plucked off and thrown away... all concerns are dead, never to be mentioned again."

George leaned back in his chair. There it was, as clear as could be..."forgiveness." He smiled to himself. Even in this culture of severe justice, the Bisorios had a beautiful expression for forgiveness.

As the missionary looked forward to teaching "God's Talk" to Mawiba, he could hardly wait to tell his friend that when God forgives sin, He says, "Nama halodaga sogao!" He plucks off sin, throws it away and all concerns and memories about it are dead, and will never be mentioned again!

* * * * * * * * * * * * * * *

About two years after they moved to Basababi, another very simple, yet incredibly significant word was eluding the missionaries...

"Have you gotten anywhere with Yanou?" George asked Bob as the two families sat together for dinner.

"No, I'm stuck!" replied Bob "I've tried to act it out and I've tried to use other words, but he just looks at me like I'm a nut! He's great in the language, but for some reason, he's not getting this one. How has it gone with you and Mawiba?"

"About the same. Man it is frustrating...we've been trying to figure out this one word for a week and a half, and haven't gotten anywhere!"

"It's such a common word," observed Harriett, George's wife, "I mean we use it all the time. We use it in recipes, it's used in math."

"We use it in our everyday speech," agreed Bob's wife, Noby, "But it's going to be vital when we tell the people the Good News."

"That's why we have to find their word for *'substitute*,'" concluded Bob. "God provided a *substitute* ram when Abraham was about to sacrifice Isaac. And Jesus is the ultimate *substitute;* giving His life for ours."

"One thing is for sure," said Harriett, "If there *is* a Bisorio word for 'substitute,' *God* knows it! Maybe we should ask Him to help us find it. I have a feeling that He is more interested in the Bisorios' salvation than we are!"

So, once again, the two couples bowed their hearts before the Master of All Languages, God Himself! They specifically asked Him to show them the Bisorio word for "substitute."

"Well, I sure hope God shows us the word pretty soon," smiled George when they had finished praying. "Otherwise, He may have to find some *substitute* missionaries for us!"

* * * * * * * * * * * * * * * *

The hunt! Some of the most exciting and interesting times for the white men were the day-long outings with the Bisorio guys, hunting wild pigs and birds. The villagers used half-starved dogs to hunt pigs; when the dogs cornered a pig, the men had to get close enough to fill the pig with arrows, and then finish it off with spears. It was a dangerous game, because an enraged boar could easily rip a man apart with his razor sharp tusks!

But on this day, they came up empty-handed! The men were tired, irritable, and *hungry!* On the way back to the village, they came upon some sago palm trees growing in a little swamp. The Bisorio word for sago is "gise." (ghee-say) They process the pulp of this tree into a tasteless, starchy paste called "sak-sak." The procedure is incredibly hard work that involves scraping, washing, sifting, kneading and cooking the pulp. If the process isn't followed properly, sago is poisonous!

The hunters were tired and weren't about to pre-pare sak-sak, but they knew that at the very top of the sago palm, at center of the trunk, there is a crunchy delicious core they call the "gise-mawi." It is edible without any time-consuming preparation. In a matter of minutes, wielding their axes with the skill of trained loggers, the Bisorios had four trees down. Then they lopped off the fronds and chopped away the outer bark with their machetes. There was enough of the "gise-mawi" for all eight of them to have a good chunk.

As they were enjoying their food, one of the men named Hameyagu piped up,

"Well, we didn't get any game today, but as a **sesa** we are eating the 'gise-mawi.'"

George and Bob stopped in mid-chew!

"Hameyagu!" they both blurted out, "What did you just say?"

He looked at them in surprise. "I said, we didn't shoot any animals, but we can eat the sago as a *sesa*."

"So, when you say *'sesa,'* you mean 'in the place of' or 'instead of,' right?" Bob and George were drilling Hameyagu with their eyes and he felt like he was under interrogation!

"What's wrong with you guys, anyway?" Said the Bisorio, "Yes, for the last time, the sago is a <u>sesa</u> for the meat we didn't get!"

The missionaries looked at one another with shining eyes. "Sesa...substitute!" But they wanted to make sure;

"Hey Hameyagu, don't get upset, but can you use *'sesa'* in any situation? I mean, could you say, Alusema bogabe *'sesa'* nama daisema bogao" ("I am using a knife to chop, <u>as a substitute for </u>chopping with a machete.")

"Well, you brainless white skins can say anything you want!" Hameyagu was trying to get Bob and George off his back, so he resorted to Bisorio ridicule! His hunting companions roared with laughter!

But the missionaries would not be put off: "Come on, Hameyagu...give us a break! We've never heard the word 'sesa' before. Listen, we might use that word when we start teaching 'God's Talk' to you guys."

That got the Bisorios' attention! After two years of living with the missionaries, they had seen good things in the hone's lives; in their marriages, in their children, in their relationships with each other. "God's Talk" seemed to be at the core of their lives, and the Bisorios were anxious to hear it. So, all of a sudden, the hunters got serious and started talking about the different ways 'sesa' could be used. As they shared, it became clear to the Americans that it could be used in a broad variety of applications. It was not restricted to food or household use. 'Sesa' could be used in a sentence with animals, people, nearly anything! Truly, 'sesa' was the Bisorio equivalent to the English word, 'substitute!'

When the hunters arrived back at the village, the Bisorio men were downcast that they had not brought home any meat. And while the missionaries shared in the disappointment of the hunt, they had something else to be very excited about: They were ecstatic that they had discovered the Bisorio word that had eluded them for nearly two weeks!

"Harriett! We found the word!" George shouted as he burst into his house.

"Noby! We found the word!" Bob shouted as he burst into his house!

The Lord of Languages had answered their prayer...again!

(4)

"Getting to the Heart"
(Spring, 1980)

Since there was a pretty strict separation of the women and men in this tribal culture, Harriett and Noby learned the Bisorio language and traditions in their interaction with the women and children in the village of Basibabi. They were constantly administering medical helps to the moms and their precious babies. In the first year, these missionary nurses had saved several newborns from death. In a short time, the infant mortality rate in Bisorio land was way down and, there were lots of healthy Bisorio kids playing in the village. Many of them were named after the missionaries! Naturally, there was an incredible bond between the white skin ladies and their Bisorio counterparts.

The men learned the language and culture by doing "guy things" with the guys, like the hunting trip where they had learned the Bisorio word for "substitute," or on hikes to neighboring villages. Now that two years had passed, the missionaries were growing pretty fluent in the language. Culturally, they were learning that the Bisorios were animistic. Their "world" was filled with spirits of dead ancestors and other spirit beings who controlled nearly everything (appendix E). In the Bisorios' minds there seemed to be no clear difference between the physical and the spiritual. But they were hesitant to share these more intimate things with the white skins; they were not ready to trust their deepest secrets with the missionaries…not yet. Thus, Bob and George were constantly looking for opportunities to gain more cultural and spiritual insight.

So, when they heard of a big gathering in another Bisorio hamlet, they were eager to go. There would be fifteen to twenty of the Bisorio men and women from Basibabi hiking for several days to take part in a "sing-sing;" an all-night dance and celebration.

"We can make the trip in four days," Hadebaiyo said with a superior grin, "But for you white skins, it will take at least eight!" (The Bisorios loved to point out to the missionaries how inept they were in their hiking skills! With their calloused bare feet and lean, wiry bodies, the Bisorios could leave the "hone" in the dust!)

On the third day of the hike, they crossed the Salumei River on a vine bridge suspended thirty feet above the water. The Bisorios call these flimsy, rope-like structures "kanda" bridges; named for *kanda,* the bamboo-like material used in their construction. The river gorge was about 60 feet wide, but this bridge, secured in the rocks of the upper banks, spanned 100 feet from end to end. After all the Bisorios had scampered across, Bob inched slowly over the raging torrent, taking baby steps on the bamboo "path" while he clutched the two shoulder-height vines to keep balance. With each step, the bridge undulated up and down. He made it across, a little shaken but unhurt.

George remained on the other side staring in horror at the tiny bridge swaying above the turbulent waters. He was absolutely petrified of heights and his heart was pounding with fear! It was a phobia he had struggled with his whole life! He prayed and prayed, begging God to give him the courage to step onto the *kanda* bridge. When he finally started across, each step was pure, quaking fear! Meanwhile, the Bisorios, who could prance like deer back and forth across the bridge, made sarcastic calls, belittling the missionary:

"What's the matter George, are you afraid of a little water?""You are nothing but a scared old lady!"

"My little girl could cross the bridge faster than you!"

"Shall we carry you, you big baby?"

Showing fear was a huge taboo for the Bisorio men. And so, having compassion for another man's fear was definitely not a big part of their culture! As these sarcastic villagers watched with glee, George inched across the swaying bridge, uttering desperate prayers each step of the way. He had to look down to be certain his feet were staying on the tiny, six inch wide, bamboo "path." But when he looked down, he saw the angry, muddy waters churning and boiling beneath him!

For the Bisorios, this was a howling good time at the expense of a cowardly white skin; but for missionary, George Walker, this was an excruciating test. In the end, it was "God's Talk" that gave him the strength to make it across. The words of the Psalmist kept filling his mind: "What time I am afraid, then I will trust in You!" (Psalm 56:3) In the middle of his fears, George found he was still able to step across the bridge, trusting in his God. When he reached the other side, he silently thanked the Good Shepherd, who had helped him "walk through the valley of the shadow of death!"

At about midday, the party came to a "cross road" in the trail. There, seated on his pack and smoking a "cigarette" of rolled wild tobacco was Bagowai, the Shaman. He had been walking since morning from his hamlet, heading to the same "sing-sing." He stood up to greet the Bisorios. As the villagers talked with the witch doctor, the missionaries were struck by his imposing figure: He stood nearly five feet, ten inches tall, almost a head taller than the average five foot, four inches of other New Guinea natives. There was an air of dignity and power about him. He was indeed "looked up to" by the Bisorios. It was obvious that they were delighted to hike the rest of the way with him: Having the witch doctor along meant that the spirits would give good travel to them.

That evening, they came to their shelter for the night; a thatched lean-to, standing on poles about six feet high. It measured about twelve feet wide by sixteen feet long. These small dwellings were built at regular intervals along some of the main trails. As many as thirty people could sleep under the thatch, packed together like sardines! (The men usually got the warm, dry spots in the center, by the fire pit!) Sleeping in these shelters without walls was common for local travelers; yet, inexplicably, as they set up camp, the Bisorios began to build walls for the shelter out of huge banana leaves.

As the light faded, Bob grabbed his flashlight to check his backpack.

"Hey, turn off the flashlight!" One of the Bisorio men yelled.

"Why? What's the problem?" Bob queried.

"The light will keep 'Duga Anege' from coming to help us."

Duga Anege—"tobacco mother." The missionaries had heard the term before. It was the name of a spirit that came upon the witch doctor and empowered him during the healing meetings that were called "babadiyao." In the past, Bob and George had always been excluded from these meetings. Bob questioned further:

"So, is there going to be a healing meeting, "babadiyao" tonight?"

"No, that's why I asked you to turn out the light!" (In Bisorio, that means, "of course, you dummy!")

"Well, could George and I join you for "babadiyao?"

There was a moment of murmuring among the Bisorios. Then the spokesman replied, "Yes. You can come."

The banana leaf walls had been added to the hut to shut out the light of the moon and stars; total darkness and complete privacy were required for the "babadiyao." George and Bob entered the dwelling and sat in the darkness with their Bisorio friends, waiting for the meeting to begin. As their eyes grew accustomed to the darkness, they noticed something that at first had been almost imperceptible; a glowing circle about the size of a quarter, floating about five feet above the floor in the darkest corner of the hut: It hovered there; a small, halo of fire. Suddenly, from the glowing ring, there came a thin, shrill voice:

"What are the white men doing here?" The ghastly voice caused Bob and George to shudder and draw closer together. They were the only white men in the hut!

"They are with us," answered some of the Bisorio men. "It's alright. Let them stay."

"It is forbidden that they witness the "babadiyao!" The voice grew even more piercing and sinister.

"But they have lived with us many moons," said the men. "They are our friends and need to learn of the healing."

"If they are here, Duga Anege will depart from Bagowai's shoulder. Then she won't be able to heal you."

"But please, Duga Anege, perhaps the white men need your healing too."

This went on for at least fifteen minutes; the voice from the little circle of fire distrusting the missionaries, and the Bisorios defending them.

Finally, the voice reluctantly consented, and George and Bob silently thanked the Lord. After two years of exclusion from "babadiyao," now they were "in."

The embers in the fire pit in the middle of the hut were nearly expired. The only light came from the small, floating, fiery circle in the corner of the hut. Suddenly, the glowing ring moved up and down in a circular motion; then it drifted from the corner, moving closer to the Bisorios who sat clustered together around the fire pit. Without warning, the ring of fire flared brighter, and the missionaries gasped; the brighter radiance now illuminated a face behind it; Bagowai; the witch doctor! He slowly stepped from the corner with a bamboo pipe in his mouth. In the tube of bamboo was a glowing ring of tobacco leaf. As he sharply inhaled, the burning tobacco flared, casting an eerie light upon his features.

The smell of burning tobacco and bamboo filled the little hut, and Bagowai beckoned to the Bisorios to approach him. Doneyaka, the woman who, two years earlier had nearly been speared by her husband, stood and stepped forward. "I have pain," she said, "here, in my stomach." She pointed to a spot near her naval, and the witch doctor bent down and touched her with the burning tobacco at the end of the pipe!

Bob and George watched with astonishment as Bagowai inhaled on the bamboo pipe. The tip glowed hot, yet Doneyaka did not flinch. Then the shaman turned to the dark corner of the dwelling. He removed his pipe and began to cough, spit and retch in the corner. As he spat, there came a rustling noise, as if small objects were dropping on the leaves on the floor. "He's spitting out the pain," thought George. "He sucked out the sickness through the bamboo, and now he's spitting it out!"

Person, after person approached Bagowai with their ailments. He "sucked out" each sickness, then coughed it up in the corner.

After an hour, nearly all of the fifteen Bisorios had their meeting with Bagowai. There was an air of mystery and power in the hut. So strong was the presence, that even Bob and George, with their logical, western minds felt it. They knew that their Bisorio friends were experiencing much more than a "doctor's appointment!" Aided by their shaman, they were entering into a world dominated by spirit beings who were the cause of all their physical misery. This "babadiyao" was indeed a profound spiritual encounter.

But, there was more. Bagowai began to groan and stagger. The bamboo fell from his hand and he crumpled and collapsed to the dirt floor. He lay on his back, quivering while the hideous voice muttered and hissed. Gradually, the trembling increased as he rocked from side to side, with the shrill voice growing ever louder. Soon, wave upon wave of spasms wracked his body, as the convulsions grew more and more violent. Finally he began flopping uncontrollably; his body thrashed and jerked, and the piercing, screeching voice babbled and screamed incoherently. Every eye was riveted on the shaman in his delirium, and the hut was filled the horrible wailing of Duga Anege. This paroxysm possessed him for several minutes, and then subsided. At last, exhaustion set in and he lay perfectly still and quiet, only his deep breathing breaking the silence.

This display of brute, spiritual power was overwhelming. For the Bisorios, there could be no doubt that Bagowai, their shaman, had done battle with the spirits of sickness. Now he lay, like a war-weary champion, completely drained after his encounter with their enemies. They needed him. And they trusted him.

Finally, after a few minutes of silence, he sat up and drew a deep breath. He knelt by the fire and blew on the embers, fanning them into flame. Then, by the light of the fire, he walked over to the corner, knelt down and scooped up something in his hands. Cupping his hands together, he came back to the center of the hut. When he opened his fingers before the fire, the silence was broken by the gasps and muffled cries of the Bisorios. For in the hand of the witchdoctor was the stuff he had sucked out of his patients: bits of glass; tiny chunks of iron; small pebbles. In their spirit world where the line between the physical and spiritual was blurred, the spell of Duga Anege held them. They believed that the spirits of suffering and sickness could use anything to cause misery. As they looked upon the hand of the shaman, the men and women clicked their tongues and shook their heads; it was no wonder they had felt such pain in their bodies.

George and Bob looked on in silence. They were experiencing a part of Bisorio culture never before seen by a westerner. These encounters with "tobacco mother," had dominated the Bisorio's lives for generations; and now, a couple of white skins were sitting in the midst of one of their healing meetings for the very first time in history! The power of the spirits was inextricably engrained in their worldview. The Bisorio men and women knew that these spirits used everything in the world to either afflict them or ease their affliction. The possibility that the witch doctor might deceive them never entered their minds. They believed that the spirits of sickness could easily use bits of glass or iron to cause pain. And they also knew that the shaman, empowered by Duga Anege, the mighty spirit of healing, could just as easily remove them. The missionaries understood that they would never be able to convince the Bisorios that it was not Bagowai, empowered by Duga Anege who had delivered them from their sickness. Witnessing this one, mighty display of spiritual power, they now understood the mastery that the witch doctor held over the people.

More importantly, they had crossed an important threshold: Trust. The Bisorios had trusted them with one of their most intimate cultural secrets. This was going to be the first of many discoveries of the spiritual forces that dominated their lives. This was the door into their hearts.

The Questions of Life

(Fall, 1980)

Gardening in the steaming jungles of Papua New Guinea is exhausting work. Temperatures regularly surpass 110 degrees Fahrenheit; with 90 to 100 percent humidity. In this sauna-like climate, the crops grow abundantly, but weed control is an endless battle. And, when your only tools are a machete and an ax, the labor in the oppressive heat is relentless.

Yet, for the Bisorios, the garden is the source of their staple foods: Sweet potatoes, corn, and taro. These starch-laden foods provide carbohydrates for life.

Taro is a solid, white, tasteless starch! It forms in the roots of a large, leafy plant. The Bisorios simply take a cutting from an existing taro plant, stick it in a mound of soil, and the leaf grows roots! In a couple of months, the roots become huge, starchy tubers.

A fourteen-year-old Bisorio boy is expected to work in the garden, not ask questions! But young Maile couldn't stop the questions that clamored in his heart:

"Why doesn't the taro plant die when I chop it off?" he wondered as he thrust cutting after cutting in the mounded soil. "How can it just grow by itself? What gives it life?" He never shared these questions with anyone; but he pondered them, turning them over in his mind. Gardening afforded time to think!

Life; the ultimate mystery: As he thought about the taro, Maile then began to think about his own life. Why was he alive? What gave him life? Then, almost against his will, he found himself approaching the terrible, dark questions of death.

Maile had been taught that when he died, his torso would decompose and become a "sowa-naga," or ancestor spirit; his ten fingernails would be "reincarnated" as parrots; and his spirit would depart to live in a "heart house" somewhere in the spirit world.

But, was this the truth? Would he find happiness in the heart house? Would he be free of the fears that plagued his life? For some reason, the traditional answers afforded him little comfort.

Maile looked at the taro plant in his hand. He shook his head and clicked his tongue. "If this plant could talk, perhaps it would answer my questions," he thought despondently. But the taro was silent; the questions of life and death remained unanswered.

Young Maile did not know that nearly everyone in his village was asking similar questions. They were trying to make sense of life. There was something about the presence of the "hone" that stirred up their uncertainties. Often, they probed the missionaries, looking for answers.

George Walker was praying and studying his Bible when he heard someone walk into the visiting room in their home. He laid down his Bible and opened the door.

"Hi Mawiba!" George said. "Good to see you. I was just reading God's Talk."

Mawiba stood in the doorway and smiled at George. The missionary knew he had something on his mind, so he invited him in and waited for Mawiba to speak. The Bisorio man sat on the floor and cocked his head to one side:

"I've been thinking," he began, "You keep talking about 'God's Talk.' And we are anxious to hear His Talk. But what about when God *looks* at you? Is it hot when He looks at you?"

"What?" George replied. He wasn't sure he had heard Mawiba correctly and was trying to process the question. But Mawiba didn't give George much time to think.

"I said, 'when God looks at you, is it hot?'"

Mawiba realized by George's blank look that he did not understand this simple question! So he patiently repeated it;

"When God looks at you, is it hot?"

Even though George understood all the Bisorio words that Mawiba was using, he had no idea what he meant, so he continued to stare at the young man in ignorance.

"Look," Mawiba continued, with a tone that he would use with a stubborn child! "When you go outside and the sun is shining, is it hot?"

"Yes, of course." George replied.

"Well, then, I am asking you," Mawiba said, as slowly as he could, "When God looks at you...IS...IT...**HOT**?!!"

Finally, it dawned on George what he was driving at. "Mawiba," he said, 'Are you asking if the sun is God?"

"Well, of course," the Bisorio man responded, "Isn't the sun the one you have come to tell us about?"

"No, Mawiba," George replied. "God is much, much bigger than the sun. The sun is tiny compared to God! God is far greater than the sun and that's why His talk is so important."

The Bisorio man looked at George doubtfully, "Well if the sun is not God, and if God is greater than the sun, He must have a really big message! You and Bob keep saying you have come to tell us this 'big' story...so go ahead, tell me some of God's talk!" Mawiba lowered his voice. "Look, there is no one else around. Just give me a little bit of the talk!"

George bit his lip. He wanted, more than anything to give his eager friend a tidbit of "God's talk." But the missionaries had determined that they would wait until they were absolutely certain they could communicate at a "heart" level before they began to teach.

"You're just going to have to wait, Mawiba," George said sincerely. "Very soon, Bob and I will be able to tell you about God. But we still don't know your tongue well enough to describe Him to you."

Mawiba shook his head and left in a huff. He was exasperated, for he had to return to his buddies and report that the hone still refused to give him any answers. "Maybe," Mawiba thought scornfully, "Maybe they really *don't* have any answers."

* * * * * * * * * * * *

Sickness: What is it? Westerners understand it to be caused by a bacteria or a virus. To a tribal person in Papua New Guinea, there is witchcraft or some malicious spirit behind nearly every sickness. Trying to keep these spirits "happy" or "appeased" was an undercurrent in the psyche of the Bisorios. The missionaries often witnessed the slaughter of pigs as sacrifices to the "Sowanaga," ancestor spirits.

As the months turned into years, the white skins learned more and more about the Bisorio view of life and death. Engrained in their minds from birth was the terror of the spirits who caused sickness and death. If the sowanaga or ancestor spirits were not to blame, there were small, vicious jungle spirits, called Yama, who shot people with their deadly bows and arrows and drank their blood! If these bloodthirsty Yama hunted you, you would surely die! The Bisorios lived in constant fear of the myriads of capricious spirits who seemed to await any excuse to cause despair.

Once a year, the Walkers and Kennells traveled downriver for a conference at the mission headquarters in the town of Goroka. This weeklong get-together with other missionaries was a time of rest and recharging. It also afforded opportunity for exchange of ministry strategies as well as a meeting place for old friends.

They usually traveled by boat and plane downriver, but in 1980 George and Bob wanted to try a new route to the yearly meeting. After studying some maps, they decided to take a 10-day hike up the mountains to a little town called Laiagam, where they could catch a truck to Goroka. "It will be a challenge and it will be fun!" The men agreed as they made their plans. "Plus, we will learn more of the language and the culture of the Bisorios along the way." Twelve of the Bisorio men, who also loved an adventure, were willing to take the white skins on the journey.

It was wise that they allowed an extra week for travel, as it turned out to be a grueling trip! Each Bisorio man carried a huge "billum;" a bag made of woven string, stuffed full of supplies. They slung these string-bags over their shoulders, packing up to fifty pounds of gear over the treacherous trails. These veterans of hiking seemed to have eyes in their feet as they strode across the slippery rocks and roots of the jungle trail without a misstep. But Bob and George had to keep their eyes riveted on the trail, watching each step lest they lose their footing on the greasy path! Jungle travel did not come instinctively to the Americans; but, since they were athletic and still in their late 20's, they managed to keep pretty good pace with the indigenous guys. There was plenty of Bisorio jesting and ridicule along the way. And, after living with these masters of sarcasm for two years, the white skins were able to "dish it out" too! So the men bantered back and forth good-naturedly on the trail. The missionaries, with their ever-present notepads, managed to write down some new names of trees and plants as they went.

Suddenly, the lead man halted, and motioned to the others to stop. Moving like a cat; slowly and stealthily to a nearby tree, his arm gradually began to extend. Then...Boom! Like a striking snake, his hand darted behind the tree and came back holding a wriggling, twelve-inch lizard by the tail!

"Whap, whap, whap!" Quick as lightning, the creature's head was bashed against the tree! This tasty morsel was then plopped into the lead man's string bag—it would serve as a delicious snack for later!

"It's like we've said before," Bob observed, "If it walks, slithers, swims or flies, it's edible!"

Seven days into the trip, the Bisorios pointed out their destination. Just visible up the mountain, still two days away, they saw a clearing in the jungle: the town of Laiagam. The missionaries were encouraged. Soon, they could catch a flatbed truck down into Goroka to meet their wives and kids who would be boating downriver to take a small plane to the conference. At this rate, they would probably beat their families to the meetings by nearly a week.

They had just resumed their trek, when they met another Bisorio coming down the trail. They could tell by his countenance that something was very wrong. The line of men clustered around him as he brought word from up the hill: Five Bisorios had died in the last week at a hamlet just four hours up the trail. None of the sacrifices to the sowanaga had worked; they had all died within two days of the first fever.

George and Bob listened to the discussion, and heard the name "Gonimai" muttered several times. "Gonimai:" the chief evil spirit. His name was seldom mentioned, but he was the cause of epidemic disease and death.

Suddenly, Yanou threw down his pack. "I'm not going another step!" he declared

"Me neither!" said another Bisorio as his string-bag hit the ground.

"Whmph! Whmph!" One by one, all the men dropped their bundles; each declaring that they had to turn back.

The white skins were stunned. "Look," said George, "We've already come three-quarters of the way. Couldn't we bypass the hamlet and still get to Laiagam?"

Yanou shook his head in disbelief. "O, so we're going to fool Gonimai, is that it? You think we're going to sneak by him?"

The other Bisorios sat down on their packs and began rolling smokes or putting wads of tobacco in their lower lips. They muttered to themselves and occasionally threw out sarcastic remarks about the insanity of even thinking about continuing the trek.

Bob appealed again; "We aren't thinking about 'fooling' Gonimai. We're just wondering if there is another route to the town."

The Bisorios were unmoved. Again Yanou spoke; "It is crazy to even go *near* there. We might as well slit our throats with our machetes! It is certain death when Gonimai hunts you! No, we will *not* keep going. If you hone are insane enough to challenge him, go ahead! But we are heading home."

The discussion was over. George and Bob knew that they couldn't finish the trip without their guides. Even if they could, the two of them traveling alone would not be safe. So, when the men finished their smokes, they all turned around and headed back down the hill. It was heart breaking for the missionaries! They looked over their shoulders one last time at the town of Laiagam, just two days off. They had struggled over brutal jungle trails for a solid week—for nothing!

The missionaries had taken this trip hoping to learn more of the thinking of their Bisorio friends; and indeed they had! They had made it to within two days of their destination and had been forced to return; not because of sickness, but because of a sadistic, powerful spirit, who hunts you and kills you at his will! This Gonimai was the same evil power who the Bisorios believed was responsible for the epidemic of deaths that had hit Basababi six months before the missionaries had come. He was not to be trifled with! The Bisorios would do anything to steer clear of him; even abandon a trip that was nearly completed.

Bob and George finally made it to the conference. They followed their families by boat and plane to Goroka. When they arrived, they retold their experience to many of their friends in the mission. That week, fervent prayers were poured out to the Lord on behalf of the Bisorio people. Only Almighty God could defeat the power of Gonimai, the evil one who held them in chains of fear.

(6)

<u>"Waiting at the Neck"</u>
(Fall, 1981)

It had been nearly three years since the Kennells and Walkers had moved into Bisorio land. Three years! The Bisorio language, that had sounded so strange and "impossible" to learn, had now become their second language. They conversed freely with the people, and the Bisorios accepted them as neighbors and even good friends.

But, to communicate the message of Jesus Christ meant speaking, not just to the mind, but also to the heart. George and Bob knew that there were other beliefs deeply rooted in the Bisorios hearts that they needed to discover before they could speak relevantly of the message of the Bible. But, over the years, little by little, the people had begun to open their hearts and share some of these traditions with the missionaries. As this day drew to its end, George Walker was visiting with Wakeya, when he was suddenly startled by his words. This

59

Bisorio leader had just used a chilling expression that was new to George.

"What did you mean, just now, when you said, 'masa hadau,' 'Waiting at the neck?' George asked, trying to hide his intense interest.

"'Waiting at the neck.'" Wakeya replied, "It is how we avenge the death of a family member. If someone causes the death, they, in turn, must die."

"Do you mean if someone *murders* your relative, then, they must die?"

"That's not what I said! Is there only one cause of death? No! There are many ways to cause death. When Geyame died, we didn't know who had worked magic on her. She began to shake and sweat and groan one night for no reason. Then, suddenly, she died. Someone had worked 'aiyago,' black magic on her, no doubt."

As Wakeya described her death, George jotted down on his pad, "Did Gayame die from malaria?"

"So," George queried, "How did you find out who worked the black magic on her and caused her to die?"

"Her family went to Bagowai, the Shaman." Wakeya replied. "The spirits revealed to him that Baso had worked magic on her. As soon as they knew, her family began to wait at the neck!"

George had to remind himself to jot down notes as he listened, spellbound by Wakeya's story. He silently thanked God that this man trusted him enough to reveal this part of their culture. He and Wakeya sat, crouched down together, looking over the Yokopas River as the evening slowly crept over the village. The setting sun cast a blood-red hue upon the water.

"Baso had no idea what was happening," Wakeya continued. Gayame's family made sure of that. They were in no hurry. They began slowly to show him special kindness. They offered him extra portions of pig meat. They encouraged their children to spend more time with his children. They were waiting…waiting at the neck!"

"Then, nine months after her death, the appointed night came. Baso, his wife and their two children were invited to a party. In the middle of the festivities, just as Baso was at the height of his mirth, Gayame's father, brothers and uncles rushed into the hut. They grabbed Baso and his family and dragged him to the middle of the hut. Then, they pinned his back against the center pole of the hut, as one of the brothers pulled his arms back behind. They tied his wrists with jungle vine to hold him tight against the pole, all the time shouting that they had come to avenge Geyame."

"But, what did he say?" Asked George. "Did he try to defend himself?"

"Of course!" Replied Wakeya. "He begged and pleaded, saying he had nothing to do with Gayame's death. It was a waste of his breath! Her family knew he was to blame…" Wakeya's voice lowered to a whisper, "Bagowai had made it perfectly clear."

A shudder ran up George's spine. He paused a moment; "What did they do next?"

"First the family pointed at him and shouted at him, recounting his offenses. Every family member had their turn to tell Baso what his crime had done to them. They told him how much they missed Gayame since she had died and how they had to avenge her death. They cursed him for the evil he had done in working 'aiyago' on her.

"Then the father, who had first right of revenge, pulled the bone dagger from his vine belt and plunged it down between Baso's collarbone and his neck. One by one, brothers and uncles stabbed him with their daggers; some behind the collarbone, some up into the armpits, some in the belly."

George was familiar with these daggers: Each was made from the thighbone of a Cassowary bird. They were deadly tools; about a foot long, hard as flint and sharp as a razor.

"But...but what about his family?" George stammered

"They had to watch without trying to rescue him. If they tried, they would be guilty of his crime, and they too would die."

George listened with horror and revulsion. It was clear that this woman had died of cerebral malaria or some other disease. Yet an innocent man was brutally murdered; his wife left a widow; his children, fatherless. All this was done in the name of justice, and all at the word of a witch doctor. It was so incredibly senseless; so cold and brutal. Yet, here was Wakeya, explaining the bloody process with no sign of emotion. Suddenly, another question came to George's mind.

"Wakeya. Have you ever "waited at the neck?"

"O, yes."

"Tell me about it."

"There is not much to tell. Ibanada, his wife and daughter all had to die. The Shaman revealed that they had worked black magic on my nephew. We waited at the neck for one month, pretending to befriend them. Then, we lured them to a feast. When they stepped out of the hut to go home, we riddled them all with arrows. They never knew what hit them. My brothers and I are very good shots."

George's throat was dry and his heart heavy. He looked at Wakeya's profile. He could see no sign of emotion on his face. George decided to risk probing into Wakeya's feelings, to try and perceive his heart.

"Wakeya," he asked, "Have you ever felt any remorse for killing that family?"

He turned and replied with a surprised look, "Why would I feel remorse? Justice had to be done!"

George dug a little deeper, "Then, tell me Wakeya, what *did* you feel?"

The sun was now nearly behind the westerly trees, and the red sunset shone on Wakeya's face.

"What did I feel...?" he repeated as he turned and stared back across the river. "I felt only terror and dread. You see, the ones we killed still had family. I feared that soon, they would "wait at the neck" for me!"

He turned and looked again at the missionary. Their eyes met. Wakeya's voice was quavering, as if his fears were rushing back upon him:

"Even though this happened many seasons ago, I *still* live in fear. Everyone in this village who has 'waited at the neck,' lives with the same terror, for death is ever stalking us! It is our bitter food, day and night!"

As George looked in the eyes of his friend, he felt the heavy oppression of this fear upon Wakeya. He had never before seen a Bisorio man admit that he was afraid. And now, the "big man" in the village was laying his heart out for this white-skin to see. George found that his revulsion was softening. As he beheld the intense fear in Wakeya's face, George found a new love and compassion growing in his heart for his Bisorio friend.

Then, as if he realized that he had shared too much, Wakeya stiffened, looked away to the south and muttered,

"Night is upon us. I must go." He rose quickly, and walked up the bank to his hut without another word.

That night, George shared the grisly story of "masa hadau," — "waiting at the neck" with his wife and fellow workers. The power of fear, and the endless cycle of revenge that enslaved the Bisorios now became crystal clear to the missionaries and it gripped their hearts. Their souls were burning with the desire to tell Wakeya and his people of the One who died on a cross to satisfy all justice: The One whose love casts out all fear. Soon, very soon, they would be able to share "God's Talk" with them.

"Help us, O Lord," they cried as they prayed together. "Give us the right words to point the Bisorios to You. O, Prince of Peace; break the power of fear and replace it with Your wonderful peace!"

We're Not Writing a PHD!

(November, 1981)

George and Bob were feeling good! They had passed their fourth language evaluation, and the language consultant from the mission had said that they were progressing well in their understanding of the Bisorio tongue. (Appendix D) After three years of being immersed in the Bisorio language and culture, they were nearly fluent in conversation and writing. But the consultant found some "holes" in their cultural understanding.

"Probably six more months of learning their culture," he had said, "Then you'll be able to begin Bible teaching."

The two missionaries were happily relating this to another consultant named Bob Gustaffson, an old friend from the mission who had come to visit them in the village. The three of them chatted in the center of the village and the talk turned to a very serious matter:

"There has been a terrible influenza outbreak way up in the mountains." George told their friend. "We've heard that over twenty Bisorios have died in the last few months."

"Yeah," Bob Kennell continued, "The sickness has really got our people worried. Well," he shrugged his shoulders, hopefully we can begin teaching in six months." At that moment, Yanou, one of the Bisorio leaders walked by.

"Hey Yanou!" Bob Kennell called out in the Bisorio tongue, "Where are you going?"

"I'm not going anywhere," he replied, "I'm staying right here until I can hear 'God's Talk!'"

Mr. Gustaffson, who did not know the language, was curious. "What did he say?"

"He said he is not going anywhere until he can hear God's Talk." Bob answered.

Bob Gustaffson looked at his two friends very seriously. He seemed struck by Yanou's reply. It was obvious that he wanted to say something, so Bob and George waited as he collected his thoughts.

"I was just thinking," he began, "thinking about the bad epidemic that is killing Bisorio people. It's possible that more of them could die."

Bob and George nodded.

"And now this Bisorio leader is saying he's not going anywhere until he hears the Word of God...."

Bob and George felt strangely uncomfortable, and nodded again.

There was a moment of awkward silence as the two missionaries looked down at their feet. Bob Gustaffson crossed his arms and gazed off into the jungle.

At last, still looking off into the bush he spoke again. "Listen guys, I don't want to meddle in your work. And I know the language consultant has his reasons. But you could be here a hundred more years and still not completely understand this culture! You came here to tell these precious people the Good News of Jesus Christ, and Yanou says he's waiting to hear the message."Then he turned to his brothers in Christ. "I don't think you should make him wait any longer!"

George and Bob were thunderstruck! A moment ago they had been happy about their progress in the Bisorio language. Now they felt strangely unhappy! Bob was right; it could take a century for complete cultural comprehension. And as George said later, "We realized we weren't doing a dissertation for a PHD!"

A fire that had been smoldering was suddenly reignited! The burning desire that had brought them from America to Papua New Guinea once again blazed in their hearts. They had become so occupied with the day-to-day struggle to master the Bisorio language and culture that they had nearly forgotten the urgency to the Gospel message! Thanks to Bob Gustaffson, they now remembered! The Bisorios needed to hear the incredible News that would transform their lives and save them from eternal death. And, they needed to hear it as soon as possible.

At the same moment in history, something was brewing that would revolutionize the methodology of New Tribes Mission. A unique plan for presenting the message of the Bible was bringing wonderful results in the Philippines. The method was quite simple in its ideology: Teach the Bible in the historical order that God gave it! , This "chronological" method starts with God's creation in the book of Genesis. So, before teaching about Jesus Christ to people who have no Bible knowledge, a "firm foundation" of Old Testament truth is first taught. (Appendix A) George and Bob had been listening to cassette tapes describing this "chronological" method just days earlier. After hearing the tapes, they had agreed that when the time came to teach the Bible to the Bisorios, they would employ this new teaching method. So, just as they discovered their method of teaching, *coincidentally* they received this challenge from their friend not to wait any longer to bring the message to the Bisorios.

Now they had the method <u>and</u> the motivation! They were really fired up!

* * * * * * * * * * * * * * * * *

After Bob Gustaffson left Bisorio country, the missionaries sent word to the mission leadership of their desire to begin teaching "God's Talk" right away. Within a few days, they received the "OK!" They were overjoyed!

They gathered the village leaders and told them it was time for them to share God's talk. Hadebaiyo rolled his eyes and said, "Well, it's about time!" Some of the men snickered, but most seemed intensely serious.

"Doge biyabenaeyo!" ("We can't delay any longer!) Yanou exclaimed. "Our people are dying without hearing 'God's talk.' You have spent way too much time all these seasons learning our speech. If you slow-tongued hone are ready to teach, we are ready to listen!"

Bob and George smiled and took the put-down graciously. They were too ecstatic about teaching to take offense! "Listen," they said, "We've noticed that it's your custom to tell your most important stories around the fires at night. So when we share God's Talk, we want to go to one hut and tell part of the story, then go to another hut and teach around that fire. We'll go from hut to hut, teaching God's talk."

The leaders looked at Bob and George in disbelief. "What do you mean, 'Hut to hut?' Is this 'God's Talk' important, or isn't it?"

"Well, of course it's important. It's the most important message you will ever hear!"

"If it is so important, forget this 'hut to hut' nonsense! You will teach the whole village at once! Let's get this 'God's Talk' out under the sun where everyone can hear it. Then we will decide if it tastes sweet or bitter!"

The white skins were amazed! A large gathering for teaching was foreign to the Bisorio culture. But the leaders were so anxious to hear the story that they were organizing an outdoor "one room school house!" Bob and George didn't want to push their good fortune, so they said, "This Talk will take many meetings. The story can't be told in a day. So shall we meet a couple of times a week for teaching?"

Again, the leaders were incredulous. "A couple of times a week? Is it important, or not? If it is so precious, you will teach us **every day of the week!"**

Now it was the missionaries who stared in disbelief. These incredible people wanted to hear the Word of God, every day! (George mused later, "In America, church-goers can't even sit through a one-hour meeting once a week!")

But was this realistic? "Listen guys," Bob said, "When are you going to get your food if we have meetings every day?"

The leaders put their heads together for a conference. After a moment of discussion, Louwa replied, "You will teach us "God's Talk" every day for five days. Then, we will spend the next two days gathering and hunting our food!"

Later that evening, George, Harriett, Bob and Noby were floating on a sea of bliss! Beyond their wildest dreams, the Bisorio people were throwing open their lives to hear the message of the Bible; "God's Talk." It seemed that the village felt as much urgency to receive the message as the missionaries felt to deliver it!

The four missionaries bowed their hearts together to give praise to the Lord:

"We thank You, Lord of heaven and earth, for granting such willingness to our friends, the Bisorios. Please open their hearts to the truth of Your Word. And give us wisdom as we teach, not just to their heads, but also to their hearts."

When they raised their heads and opened their eyes, the Walkers and Kennells looked upon each other with love and gratitude. George and Harriett were from New Jersey, Bob was from California, and Noby was from Hawaii. Yet, the Sovereign Lord of the universe had brought these couples and their children from "far down river" to this distant land called Papua New Guinea. Now, after three and a half years together, these two families found that they had truly become one.

They sat together, enjoying the presence of the Lord and anticipating the opportunity to teach the Word of God to the Bisorios when a memory suddenly came to George's mind:

"It just struck me," he said, thinking out loud, "Four years ago, I was on the brink of turning around. Just a tiny change of decision, and Harriett and I would not even *be* here today!"

He returned to his memories and saw himself four years earlier, in a little apartment in New Jersey, preparing to pour out his heart to his wife....

(8)

The Power of Choice

(December, 1977)

Harriett Walker, now seven months pregnant with their first child, sat on the couch in their apartment in New Jersey, waiting for her husband to speak his mind.

"Come on, George," she finally blurted out, "Tell me what's wrong."

George took a deep breath and began slowly,

"Honey, I don't know how to tell you this, but, well, I'm scared to death…I don't think I'm ready to take this step…Maybe we should wait a year before we go to Papua New Guinea…"

"Oh my goodness, George! What in the world are you talking about? We've already got our tickets! We're leaving in a week…Are you crazy?"

"Harriett, I know all that. But look at me…I'm a lousy husband, I have no idea how to be a father… and look at where we are going. We will be isolated from family and friends for four or five years at a time in one of the most primitive countries in the world. Harriett, think of all the diseases; malaria, yellow fever...we could die! We could be killed by hostile tribal people...we could even be eaten by cannibals!"

"What has gotten into you, George? We have been in training for four years and have considered the dangers again and again. I thought we had decided that we would follow the Lord wherever He led us."

"Well, yeah we decided...but maybe He's not leading us! Maybe we are deceiving ourselves and heading off to who-knows-where just to die in the jungle somewhere!"

"I can't believe I'm hearing this, George. We know that God has not given us the spirit of fear. Either Satan is throwing these uncertainties at you, or, well...you're listening to your own doubts."

They continued their discussion far into the night. Finally, George subdued his fears enough to agree to go. If the truth was to be known, he only gave in because his pride kept him from admitting his anxieties to the rest of his family. Plus, he knew that they were being supported by lots of Christians; how could he tell them that he was going to quit before he even started? Then, there were the wonderful members of their local church who were so excited to help send them on the mission field. How would he ever be able to look them in the eye if he gave up? At this point, only embarrassment and shame kept him on the path to Papua New Guinea.

On a cold January 1st, 1978, the Walkers found themselves at the Philadelphia Airport preparing to depart, first to Los Angeles; then, hopping from island to island in the Pacific, on to Papua New Guinea.

There was a huge crowd gathered to see them off. As George looked upon his friends and family, his fears and anxieties again began to rise. As he talked with his pastor, he glanced over at his parents and saw his mother weeping and sobbing. His father stood by her with tears running down his cheeks.

Suddenly, she stood up from her chair and walked over to her son. To George's chagrin, she threw her arms around his neck and sobbed,

"Oh, George! If I have ever done anything wrong...if I've been a bad mother, please forgive me...forgive me, son, forgive me, I'm so sorry...."

George assured his mom that there was nothing to forgive, but his mind was steeped in incredible apprehensions; what was this outburst from his mom all about? He felt like he was going to the gallows!

As he hugged his mom, he noticed his father, now standing behind her. His face was smeared with tears and he whimpered to himself, "It isn't fair...it isn't fair...." It was tough enough trying to deal with his mother's sorrow. But now, his dad was mourning too...George's emotions were clawed to shreds and his resolve to go was hanging by a thread!

Before boarding the plane, the wonderful folks from the church made a big circle with the Walkers in the center. They smiled and sang, "God be with you 'til we meet again." It was a sweet and heartfelt goodbye from a very supportive fellowship. But to George, it sounded like a funeral dirge!

He thought to himself, "That's easy for you guys to sing, but you're not traipsing across the world to die in the rainforest! How can you be so presumptuous? How in the world do you know if we'll *ever* 'meet again?' None of the well wishers at the airport had a clue what was happening in his heart. But as the reality of departing was upon him, George Walker was absolutely terrified.

"I'm sorry folks," said the airline representative, "But it's time to board the plane." After final goodbyes, the Walkers took their seats on the airliner. As the plane lifted from the Philadelphia airport, George looked out the window in a dark cloud of depression and fear. "What in the world am I doing?" He wondered. "I can't leave."

During that long flight across country, George once again unloaded on his poor, pregnant wife! He poured out his fears, doubts and uncertainties with renewed passion. He felt like a caged animal, trapped into doing something that scared him to death. Worse than that, he knew he was an absolute hypocrite! He was supposed to be a missionary, going to tell the Good News to people who had never heard. But he was so filled with his own fears that he really didn't care about the eternity of others.

By the time they arrived in Los Angeles, George had nearly driven Harriett to distraction! They deplaned and Harriett threw herself into an airport chair. "Look George," she said in utter exasperation, "You know that I am totally committed to this ministry. We have been working and studying and saving and planning for this very day. This is our dream come true. But now, you make it sound like a nightmare! You have got to make up *our* mind! Are we going, or aren't we?"

George paced back and forth in front of his wife. Then he stopped and pointed to the row of pay phones on the wall opposite them. "O.K!" he declared, "This is it! I'm going to pick up one of those phones, dial our pastor and tell him the truth. I'm going to tell him that George Walker is a fake and a phony and has no business going on the mission field!"

Harriett looked upon her husband with tearful resignation. "All right, if that's your decision, then go ahead and get it over with."

He walked toward the phones, but, as if to avoid the excruciating talk with his pastor, he kept walking and found himself standing in a ticket-booking line. He decided to talk to a ticket agent about a return flight to Philadelphia.

As he waited in the line, this fearful young man began to sense that he wasn't alone. The hustle and bustle of the airport seemed to fade into the background and he felt the Presence of the One he loved best..."George; haven't I proven Myself faithful to you?"

No, it wasn't an audible voice. Nevertheless, in the midst of all his fears, George found himself listening to his Lord and Master; "I have kept you and Harriett on this path to the mission field for these last four years, haven't I?" George nodded his agreement.

"And you know, my son, that if you turn around now, you won't be able to tell anyone that it was I who sent you back." Again, George found himself agreeing with the Lord."

"Trust Me, my beloved. In the midst of your fears, trust Me. I have been faithful to you and I will continue to be faithful to you. Don't turn around now before you have even started. Trust me."

"May I help you sir?" George was startled from his conversation with the Lord. He was now standing before the smiling ticket lady! He looked at her sheepishly and then replied, "Uh, well, no…No thank you. I guess I've made up my mind."

He quickly stepped out of the line, leaving a very bewildered travel agent behind!

George strode back across the terminal to his bride. She looked up, wiping away a tear as he approached. "Well, George, did you book us tickets back to Philadelphia?"

"No, babe, I didn't. Listen, I know I'm looking like a double- minded man here, but while I was waiting in line, I made up my mind. We're going forward. The Lord is faithful. He will take care of us."

Harriett looked at her husband for a moment. "So, we're staying on track; we're going to Papua New Guinea?"

"That's right. The Lord showed me that if we quit now, we wouldn't be able to say that God sent us back. I've just got to trust Him in the middle of my fears."

"So, we're going. You're sure."

"Yes, we're going."

"You've made up your mind."

"Yes, I've made up my mind."

"No turning back?"

"No turning back!"

Harriett, once again studied her husband's face. "OK, babe," she finally said. "This is it! We are going to get on that plane to Hawaii, and we are going all the way to Papua New Guinea! I don't want to go through this again in Honolulu!"

The Walkers *did* board that plane to Hawaii! And, they did, indeed make their way to Papua New Guinea. Then, less than 6 months later, they moved with their baby boy into Basababi; the main village of the Bisorio people.

* * * * * * * * * * *

Now, four years later, the Walkers and their co-workers, the Kennells were preparing to teach "God's Talk" to their friends, the Bisorios!

George's thoughts returned to the present. It was another hot, humid night in the Sepik region of Papua New Guinea. And four missionaries were sitting together in a little bush house, thousands of miles from their homeland. In spite of the fears and doubts of four years ago, here he was!

"Whew, that was close!" he said as he shook his head, "I am so glad I didn't turn back at the Los Angeles airport!"

(9)

<u>Under the Sun!</u>
(October, 1981)

Kabalame and Doneyaka sat before the morning fire, which crackled in the fire pin in the center of their hut. The smoke gathered beneath the blackened underside of the grass roof; then it finally filtered through the thatch into the morning air. Looking across the fire pit, Kabalame noticed his wife's smile as she prepared the sweet potatoes.

"Hamege beme budubudubane?" ("Why are you so happy?") he asked.

She glanced up at her husband. There was something different in his voice. He wasn't asking in his usual sarcasm; he seemed genuinely interested.

"I'm happy," she replied, "because today we will hear this talk about God."

"But why would that make you happy?"

"Because, I have seen true happiness in the white skins. I think they are happy because of their God."

Kabalame looked thoughtfully at the fire. "When the "hone" first came I didn't trust them. But I too have seen their happiness. And I have seen much more. I have seen them heal our babies . . . and us. And though I have ridiculed their slow tongues, I have watched them working hard to learn our speech. They have come from far downriver, leaving their big houses to live with us." He hesitated, as if he was struggling with the words. "So, now I *do* trust them. They have proven to me that they really care for us."

Doneyaka, seeing her husband's tender mood, risked sharing another thought; "We women have noticed something else, and we have talked about it very much." She paused, knowing that the men usually didn't care what the women thought. But, he was listening, so she continued; "We have seen that the white skin men have a deep care . . . a deep *love* for their wives. Perhaps," she said slowly, "it is because of their God that they have this love."

She looked down and continued the food preparation. "Yes, I have waited many moons to hear this God's Talk!" (Appendix B)

If the Bisorios were anxious to hear the talk, the missionaries were incredibly eager to "talk the talk!" After three and a half years of living in the steaming jungle of Papua New Guinea, the day they had been dreaming of had arrived! That first morning of teaching dawned bright and sunny. Truly, this new message would be "under the sun," just as the Bisorios requested! A hill in the center of the village became the meeting place. The Kennell's home was just below the hill and the missionaries met there regularly to pray for each of their Bisorio friends by name.

"Hey George," Bob called across the room, as they finished praying about their first day of teaching, "I just thought of something."
"What's that, Bob?' George replied.
"I just realized that if I hadn't moved here, I could be back in America doing something important, like watching T.V!"
George laughed, "Yeah, who would want to come to the rainforest to do something as petty as this?"
Suddenly, their mood changed as the deep significance of the coming days settled upon them. "Man...this is it; this is really it!" reflected Bob. This is the very reason we came."
"I feel overwhelmed," replied his co-worker. "I'm torn between ecstatic joy and incredible fear. Yes, this is the reason we came. I just pray that God will be glorified as we try to proclaim Him to our Bisorio friends."

Thirty-five men women and children gathered together that first morning, eager to hear the message. They sat in a semi-circle on top of the hill as the missionaries proclaimed the message of the Bible. This began a daily ritual that would last for five months! Bob and George had spent many late nights preparing Bible lessons. And, thanks to the efforts of Harriett and Noby, there were already about a dozen Bisorios who were learning to read and write their own language. Very soon, as they became more literate, they would be able to review the lessons after the teaching times.

"In the beginning, God created the heavens and the earth."

Since the Bible starts with God, that's where the missionaries started! The Bisorios believed that the sun, the sky and the "ground" had always existed. They thought that the sun, a fiery, powerful spirit being, had somehow created all life, including all the other spirits. Now, the missionaries held before them Someone super-personal, Someone immense, who existed before the earth, the sky, and even the sun.

George and Bob looked upon the attentive faces of their friends. They felt a huge joy, yet a great responsibility; they were representing Almighty God!

"God had no beginning," Bob proclaimed, "And He will have no end! He has no father and He has no mother!" He paused, as the concept of "Eternality" sunk in to the Bisorios. " "Yes," he continued, "God alone is eternal and all other things have their beginning in Him!"

Then, as the Bisorios watched, George stretched out his hands and pointed east and west; "From the everlasting vanishing point to the everlasting vanishing point, He is God! And it is He who created the earth and sky. Listen Bisorios! God is the One who created the sun! The sun is not personal and has no will to create. Only this magnificent, all powerful God can bring things into being."

Sixteen year old Maile sat, spellbound. Of course, of course! The Creator of life had to have life *in Himself* in order to grant life to the created things! "The taro that I plant in the garden…the Living God gives it life! It should die when I cut the shoot from the plant, but it grows new roots. God, the Creator, grants life to the new plant!"

God, the Creator: Personal; Powerful; Immense; Loving; Eternal! These are the attributes drawn from the Bible that the missionaries proclaimed. As the truth was proclaimed, the sun was "overshadowed" by Almighty God! The sky was put "under" the Lord who is above all! And the earth became mere "dust" in His creative Hand!

They spent the first several days proclaiming this Almighty Creator. He is Immortal, Invisible; In His essence, He is Spirit, having no body. He is loving, merciful, just and holy.

After describing His eternal attributes, the missionaries launched into a two week teaching celebration of the seven days of creation! They followed the Biblical pattern, carefully describing the plants and animals known to the Bisorios and ascribing their creation to Almighty God. The men and women were so riveted by these new concepts that they sent word to the outlying hamlets, beckoning their kin to come hear the teaching. By the end of the creation account, the "congregation" had grown from thirty-five to fifty!

As Creator-God captivated the minds of the Bisorios, He became the "talk of the town!" They began to give Him credit for all they saw. The rolling clouds or a flock of birds overhead would produce exclamations of; "Oi dae, Oi dae! Godema na Gode hadaowaga dawamo!" (Look, look! God is showing us that He is God!")

Yes, God was looming far greater than anything the Bisorios had ever imagined! Creation was coming to life, for the truth was hitting home in their hearts. They were beginning to "bow the knee" before God, their Creator.

(10)

The Entrance of Evil

(November, 1981)

"If God is good, and His creation is good, why is there so much bad in our lives?" This was the question that now pressed upon all the Bisorios. Over the next several days of teaching, the missionaries probed that very question!

"Can you imagine an incredible garden, loaded with fruit and vegetables, but no weeds?" Bob and George knew this would grab their attention!

No Weeds! The missionaries described this beautiful place called the Garden of Eden and the Bisorios were spellbound. Their very lives depend upon gardening, so the first Garden in the Bible was a beautiful mystery to the Bisorios; what a paradise!

"Think of it," George continued, "An absolutely beautiful place with an abundance of food to eat; no back-breaking toil; no thorns; no wild pigs rooting up the garden! All of it created by God for man to enjoy! What a wonderful place it must have been."

There was excited chatter among the people as they contemplated the perfect paradise called Eden. Mawiba jumped up in the middle of the discussion and spoke for the whole group, "Where is this place? Have you guys seen it? We would give everything we own to move into that perfect garden!"

"I'm sorry, Mawiba," Bob replied, "We have never seen it. It is gone. Something went terribly wrong and the paradise has been lost."

Mawiba threw himself back down to his seat, "I knew it," he grumbled to himself. "It was too good to be true. That beautiful place; someone messed it up."

Then, the excitement turned to sadness and frustration as the Bisorios realized that Eden was no more. Yanou shook his head in anger, "O, I'd like to get my hands on the guy who wrecked it! If I got a hold of him, I would chop him into tiny pieces with my machete!"

A good world that has gone wrong...that is the biblical picture of our world. And the chief proponent of the "wrongness," is a terrible creature that the Bible calls Satan! Before talking about Adam and Eve, the missionaries taught on the creation of angels, and the chief angel, Lucifer. The Bisorios clearly realized that the angels were created in goodness, but, a third of them fell into pride and followed Lucifer in his rebellion against God. They agreed that God was right and just to judge them and prepare a lake of fire for their punishment.

Finally, with the creation of the angelic hosts as a foundation, the missionaries taught on the creation of man. For the first time in their history, the Bisorios learned that there was dignity in their human-ness: Created in the image of God!

"Mankind was created in God's image...made to worship and serve their Creator and delight in a happy relationship with Him!" The "white-skins" gladly proclaimed God's purpose for making man. They were about to continue, but hesitated; there was a blank stare in nearly every Bisorio! Something had grabbed their thinking, and they were no longer listening to the missionaries.

This was a signal to the teachers to give the "students" time to talk amongst themselves! So Bob encouraged the people: "Go ahead and talk together; what do you think of when you hear that God's purpose for creating man was to have a relationship, even a friendship with him?"

This was entirely new territory for the Bisorios, and they had trouble wrapping their minds around the concept: "God made us to enjoy a *relationship* with Him?" Hadebaiyo and Yanou were flabbergasted! .... "We *can't* have a relationship with the sun! And we wish the spirits would help us in our hunting, but then leave us alone! We have only fear of the spirits. But, Almighty God desires a *relationship* with *us?*" The two men wrestled in thought, back and forth, examining this mind-bending idea.

87

"How could the Creator look at us as His friends?" Doneyaka asked her girl friend. "He is so High, so Good, so Pure. How would He ever have a desire for that kind of relationship?"

The talk among the Bisorios went on for twenty minutes; and all the conversations ran down the same two tracks: 1) Utter *amazement* that Creator-God made man for relationship with Him, and 2) Stark awareness that none of them were enjoying this relationship with God!

The next day, Bob and George continued to paint the picture of Eden: Man and woman in harmony with one another and with their Creator; complete freedom to tend their world and to fellowship with their Lord; and, moral accountability to obey God in the simple commands He gave them.

"Since we are made in the image of God, we have the freedom to choose the path we walk. Adam and Eve were also given this freedom, to choose to follow God, or choose to go their own way! God made it clear that to disobey Him meant death."

Then, using drama, they pictured the temptation of man by the enemy of their souls, Satan. This was a gripping portrayal for the people, for they truly saw themselves in Adam and Eve. They understood that the happiness of the whole human race was somehow tied to this pivotal discourse between the serpent and Eve.

"Did God really say you must not eat from *any* tree in the garden?" Satan twisted God's statement to Adam and Eve, and the Bisorios saw it immediately!

"That's not what God said!" shouted Mawiba.

"Don't listen to him, he's a liar!" called out Yanou.

The missionaries had trouble acting out the story because the Bisorios kept interrupting the drama to cheer on their "parents," Adam and Eve!

Finally, the serpent enticed Eve, and the villagers watched in agony as she and Adam ate the forbidden fruit! O, what a terrible moment in man's history! Then they watched as the Lord came on the scene to pronounce judgment on His wayward children.

DEATH! The thing most feared by man; and the curse that haunted the lives of the Bisorios. Spiritual and physical death came upon the whole race because of Adam's sin.

"Do you see what Satan did?" George wanted to use something from the Bisorio's culture to drive it home to them, "He deceived Eve, making himself look like her friend. And all the time he was luring her to her death. Don't you see...Satan WAITED AT THE NECK for Adam and Eve! Yes, he pretended to be their friend, when all he really wanted was their physical and spiritual death!"

"But there is a big difference," Bob continued, "between your "waiting at the neck" and Satan's. When you fool someone into his death, he has no choice in the matter! But when Satan tempted Adam and Eve, they freely *chose* to disobey God and bring death upon themselves and upon all their offspring, including us!"

Because of their deep understanding of the connection of forefathers to their offspring, the Bisorios had no problem seeing that Adam's sin and punishment would come upon them as well! But Bob and George wanted to make sure that the people couldn't "weasel out" of their guilt.

"Don't think that you will escape God's judgment because you were not the ones in the Garden of Eden! Just think of all the times you yourselves have disobeyed the Lord! But now you can see that death does not come because of the arrows of the yama! No! Death comes because man disobeyed the clear and simple command of the Lord."

As Bob and George taught about God's personal judgment on Adam, Eve and the Serpent, conviction fell upon the Bisorios. They were no more able to hide from the gaze of God than Adam and Eve had been able to hide in the Garden!

The missionaries made sure that the villagers understood the significance of the Lord providing animal skins as a covering for man: First of all, man's attempt at making his own covering of fig leaves was ineffective to cover his nakedness...only God could provide them with a covering; Secondly, an innocent animal had to die before God could cover the nakedness of Adam and Eve. This was the first teaching on the shedding of blood for the forgiveness of sin. This theme would be revisited again and again in the next months of teaching.

At this juncture of the teaching, the Bisorios began to despair. They knew they were as guilty of rebelling against God as their mother and father,

Adam and Eve! But, following the pattern of scripture, Bob and George introduced the "Promised Deliverer," first mentioned in Genesis 3:15:

"Don't despair friends!" shouted Bob. "God gave hope to Adam and Eve, and there is hope for you."

"That's right," continued George, "The Lord said that the 'seed of the woman' would come and crush the serpent's head! He would destroy the works of Satan and make a way for man to get back to God!"

When the seated men and women heard this news, an excited undertone buzzed through the crowd. Faces that had been downcast now wore smiles and the murmur rose to an outcry:

"Well then, tell us, has this Deliverer been sent? Who is He? If He hasn't been sent, when will He be sent?"

"O yes," the missionaries responded, "God has already sent the Redeemer and we came all the way from America to tell you the Good News of His coming."

Again, the Bisorios talked in hushed excitement. Suddenly, one of the women named Enome shouted out, "I know, I know! Bob and George, *you* are the ones God promised to send! Are you *both* the Promised Deliverer?"

George and Bob burst into laughter. "Please, please, you guys," they said in their amusement, "You should know us well enough by now that we couldn't be the Deliverer! And you should be very glad that we aren't!

But He truly is the reason we have spent all these years living among you and learning your language. If you will keep listening, very soon we will talk about this Wonderful Redeemer and the way He cut a path to the Lord."

This foretaste of the Good News was just what the Bisorios needed to hear! One of their leaders named Daniya, stood to his feet and exhorted his countrymen,

"Listen, my brothers," he cried, "This 'God's Talk' is really important. This is really good talk! We not only need to come to the lessons; we need to be talking about it wherever we go! We need to discuss it in our gardens, in our houses, and on the foot paths. We need to talk about it when we get up in the morning and when we go to sleep at night!"

The missionaries stood before the people astounded. One of their own leaders had practically quoted the book of Deuteronomy! (Without ever hearing it!) And as they looked at each face, they saw heads nodding in agreement. The incredible importance of "God's Talk" was grabbing all their hearts.

(11)

Conflict and Confusion

(February, 1982)

"**I** am so amazed at how well the teaching is going," remarked George as he and Bob prepared for the day's lesson.

"Me too," Bob replied, "The people are so attentive and responsive. It's almost too good to be true!"

They headed out of the Kennell's house up to the "teaching hill," and as they got to the top, they saw two groups of Bisorios seated on the ground, facing each other. This was the typical setting for tribal "court." (Appendix C) Two clans were arguing over the price of the bride that Hameyagu wanted to purchase. The missionaries sensed the heat of the discussion as they approached: Apparently, not many folks in the woman's clan were in favor of Hameyagu's intentions and they just wanted to end the deliberation;

"I think you all ought to just leave the village," Blurted out Yanou, speaking for the woman's family. "If Hameyagu and his line (clan) would just get out of here, the problem would be over!" That brought a loud response from the other side! The intensity of the "discussion" was definitely stepped up a notch!

After listening a moment, the Americans spoke up;

"Hey you guys, it's time for our teaching. Why don't you continue this after our session."

The Bisorios grumblingly agreed and turned to face the missionaries for the Bible lesson. Bob and George continued to teach on the consequences of Adam and Eve's rebellion, and the clear division between their offspring who willingly followed God, and those who continued to follow Satan.

After the teaching, the Bisorios immediately resumed the "marriage court!" Unlike yesterday, today their hearts had not really been in the Bible lesson! Yanou began rolling a "smoke" and started bantering again about the other "side" moving out of Basababi. Yanou was a real talker, but in this discussion he seemed to blabber unceasingly!

"Boy, he's going on forever!" thought George as he listened to Yanou. Others were thinking the same thing!

"Give someone else a chance to talk!" yelled one of Hameyagu's relatives.

"They're right!" shouted Hadebaiyo. "You've talked way too long!" Though he was Yanou's brother, he was fed up with his endless chattering.

Yanou was oblivious to these comments, and kept throwing verbal insults at the other clan. He was wound up and seemed intent on dominating the discussion.

"Shut up!" yelled Hadebaiyo again as his anger rose, "You've repeated yourself a hundred times!"

Yanou responded by talking even louder!

By now, Hadebaiyo was livid. He jumped up, pounded his feet in rage and ripped off the shirt he was wearing. Then he balled up the shirt, threw it to the ground and charged at his seated brother. He took a roundhouse swing at Yanou as he rushed upon him. But Yanou saw the blow coming and ducked. Hadedbaiyo missed him completely and flew by!

Yanou laughed as his brother ran by, and continued jabbering at the "other side."

Hadebaiyo turned on his heels, and rushed back at his brother. This time, coming from behind, he smashed him with his clenched fist upside the head and sprang past him!

Yanou, was momentarily shaken, but pretended to be unaffected by being clobbered! He laughed and shook his head, acting as if nothing had happened. Hadebaiyo stood breathlessly watching his brother, when suddenly, Yanou's smiling countenance contorted into raging anger and he jumped to his feet! He screamed and cursed at his brother, threatening to beat him to death. Then he wheeled around and raced down the hill toward the Kennell's home. Hadebaiyo, itching for a fight, was hot on his heels.

"I'll kill him! I'll crush his empty head!" Yanou screamed as he reached the Kennell's house and picked up a wooden pole leaning against the wall.

He whirled around to club his brother, but Hadebaiyo saw the blow coming and with one motion grabbed another post and swung it with all his might! The two staffs crashed together with an ear splitting, "Crack!"

Then, like a couple of sword fighters, they were at it, "hammer and tongs;" swinging the clubs furiously at each other. Meanwhile, the hilltop was emptied as the villagers rushed down from the meeting place to see the battle! Finally, Yanou threw his post at his brother and sprinted toward his hut; he was after his ax! Hadebaiyo began to pursue him, but several of the men tackled him and wrestled him to the ground.

Another group of men chased after Yanou. He was already inside his hut when they arrived, so Bob Kennell threw the door shut and leaned against it, holding it with his hands. The door was made of very thin wood, but he hoped to trap Yanou long enough for him to cool down a little. Two other Bisorio men also threw their weight against the door.

"I'll kill him!" Yanou roared again from inside his hut. Then, without warning, the door jolted, and splinters exploded right in Bob's face! He sputtered and blinked. There, only one-half inch from his thumb, he saw an ax-head sticking through the wooden door! Yanou was going to chop his way out to get to his brother!

Realizing that his position was decidedly unsafe, Bob threw his hands off the door and leapt back. At that instant, the crazed Bisorio with ax in hand rocketed out the door; right into the arms of his countrymen! Bob jumped in, and there was a brief but

violent wrestling match. Quickly, Yanou was subdued and the ax was wrenched from his hands. He
lay writhing and cursing on the ground held by three
other Bisorios and missionary, Bob Kennell.

The rest of the day was basically, "guard duty"
for the whole village. The two murderous brothers
were kept apart and all their tools and weapons
were taken from them. Meanwhile, the "town-talk"
concerning a wife for Hameyagu continued in all its
intensity. With the real prospect of bloodshed upon
them, many more of the Bisorios were advocating
sending a large group away to end the marriage
talks, and to avert slaughter in the village. The Bible
teaching had been going so well, but now it seemed
that the village was about to explode! As evening
wore on, the four missionaries gathered together to
talk and pray about the incredibly volatile situation.

While they talked, some of the men came to the
door. They looked nervous and uneasy. "We think
that Yanou has hidden a bone dagger under his
grass skirt." they said. "We're afraid he's planning
to butcher Hadebaiyo in his sleep."

"Tell Yanou that we want to see him right away!"
said Bob, "Tell him it is extremely important."

The men hurried off to relay the message. In
a few minutes, they returned with Yanou. He also
appeared upset, but was trying to act noncha-
lant. Bob and George chatted with him for a few
moments; then Bob set his jaw and said,

"Yanou, listen. If I ask you a question, will you
promise to tell me the truth?"

"Sure, Bob," he replied, I have always told you the truth."

"O.K., great. Then please tell me what you have hidden in your grass skirt?"

"Well, um...nothing! I'm not hiding anything!"

"Now, Yanou, remember; you promised to tell the truth. I can see that you are hiding something. Could it be that you have a 'daise' under your belt?"

"O...That!" He looked down and pulled out the knife, "I had completely forgotten I had it with me!"

George and Bob eyed the guilty man briefly; then George spoke up,

"Yanou, what were you planning to do with the 'daise?'"

"I wasn't planning anything! I told you, I forgot I even had it!"

"Could it be," George persisted, "that you were thinking about using it on your brother?"

"No way! I'm not even upset any more." His shifting eyes were saying the exact opposite!

"Well, if that's the case," Bob continued, "Give us the dagger to keep for you tonight. We really wouldn't want you to do something that you would regret."

"O, really, that's not necessary. I'm not angry at all!"

"Then, if you're not mad, and not planning on using the dagger, there should be no problem in letting us have it!"

The argument went on for a few more minutes until, reluctantly, Yanou turned the bone dagger over to the missionaries. Though he continued to deny it, it was obvious that he was still furious with

Hadebaiyo. After he left, the two couples clasped hands around the kitchen table and cried out to the Lord. The situation was indeed desperate.

But, even as they prayed, a plan for the next day was growing in their hearts.

There was an uneasy peace among the Bisorios the next morning. They knew that any bloodshed would scare the white skins and possibly make them leave the village. So they tried to smooth over the conflict. Hadebaiyo and Yanou had cooled down during the night, but still, the tension was brewing just below the surface. The spirit of murder seemed to be brooding over Basababi.

The villagers gathered for the morning teaching and sat in their usual spots "under the sun," at the top of the hill. But, the missionaries were absent. This was very strange....

"Look! What is it? What's happening?!" cried out one of the ladies as she jumped to her feet, covered her mouth in fear and pointed down the hill. All heads jerked around, and every eye opened wide, for they saw the source of her fear:

Ascending the hill were two ghostly-looking figures. They walked slowly, sadly, painfully. The morning sun shone down on them and revealed a dusty, light-yellow hue to their skin. Clad only in their shorts, and covered from head to toe in dried, yellow mud, George and Bob walked up sadly toward the awaiting Bisorios.

They reached the teaching spot, then stood silently before the crowd, looking sorrowfully from face to face. At last, the Bisorios could stand it no longer:

"Why are you covered in the silt of mourning?" Louwa asked. "Has someone died?"

"We heard of no death during the night," said Wakeya, "What is the meaning of this symbol of grief?"

Bob spoke first: "O, dear friends. We are mourning because we know that many of you are not only going to die; but die and go to the place of fire."

"But you said you would give us the Good News that would spare us from God's judgment," objected Louwa. "You are going to tell us of the Promised Deliverer."

"Yes, and we want to tell you the Good News," said George, "But we have heard that many of you Bisorios are going to be sent away. If you leave the village, you will never hear the Good News of God's talk; you will not be able to believe it and be saved."

While the men were reasoning with the people on the teaching hill, their wives were on their knees in their homes, pleading with Almighty God to work in the hearts of the people. The future of the work was hanging in the balance, with the village about to disband. This was intense spiritual warfare, and Harriett and Noby fervently interceded for their husbands and for the Bisorio people they had come to love so much.

"We are truly in mourning!" continued Bob, "Yes, we went down to the river's edge at dawn to smear ourselves in your traditional "coat of grieving," because we can see that all of you are playing right into Satan's hands! He is deceiving you; causing this fighting and division. He doesn't want you to hear God's Talk because he wants to take you to the place of fire where he is going! Our hearts are broken because we don't want to see any of you lost for eternity! This is why we are mourning!"

As the missionaries pleaded with the people, they saw encouraging signs: Heads were bowing and wagging from side to side; many tongues clicked in agreement with what they had said; "It's true, it's true," was the murmur from the crowd, "We have listened to Satan," they admitted.

When the Bisorios acknowledged their wrong, a wave of tranquility seemed to sweep over the whole village. Somehow, Yanou and Hadebaiyo let go of their grievances with one another. It was as if they awoke from a dream and realized that they needed this "God's Talk" much more than they needed to seek revenge on each other. In a culture that was ruled by vengeance, this was completely unheard of.

Even more amazing than the peace between the two brothers was the change in Hameyagu; for he and his clan did not pursue the plan to buy him a wife! His desire to hear the Word of God was so strong, that when he saw that the teaching was in jeopardy, he dropped his pursuit of a mate! His unselfish act did more to bring peace than anything the missionaries could have said.

The next morning, when Bob and George arrived for teaching, instead of finding a smaller crowd, the numbers had actually grown! Miraculously, the Spirit of God poured His peace upon this isolated corner of His creation.

The plans of the enemy had been thwarted!

(12)

The Justice of the Almighty

(March, 1982)

The history of mankind as recorded in the Bible is not very pretty! After Adam and Eve fell into sin, most of their offspring followed their sinful hearts and turned their backs on God. The missionaries in Bisorio-land didn't try to soften the bleak facts, but they always held out the hope that a Deliverer was coming, just as God had promised. The Old Testament stories were chosen to teach the sinfulness of man and the justice of God. But God's wonderful mercy was always included.

The Bisorios now understood their connection to all mankind through Adam. And they freely accepted their sinfulness; not just because of Adam's choice, but due to their own rebellion against God! The story of Noah and the ark was particularly gripping to them as they saw the hardheartedness of mankind:

"Imagine a huge boat in the middle of dry land!" The missionaries tried to picture the ark; its immensity and its purpose. "It had to be large enough to house a male and female of all the animals. But, it was nowhere near a river or the ocean!" Using skits, George and Bob tried to dramatize Noah's situation:

"Hey Noah! Are you planning on doing some fishing in the middle of this field!" George played the part of the mocking crowds; "What's all this talk about some sort of 'judgment from God!' Water falling from the sky? Bah! We don't believe in God. And even if He did exist, He'd never judge us!"

"But He *will* judge you, and the judgment is coming soon!" Bob, playing the part of Noah, the 'preacher of righteousness,' thundered out the message of God's justice: "If you don't trust the Lord, believe His word, and take His way of escape, you will perish in your sins! The flood is coming! Come and join us! Confess your sins to the Lord and be forgiven. Then help us make the ark ready."

"You're a religious fanatic!" the mocker replied. "I love my lifestyle and I'm not going to let your God meddle in my life. Besides, why would God judge me? I'm as good as the next guy! Take your boat, and go paddle it somewhere else!"

The white skins used a number of skits, teaching on the sinfulness of man in Noah's day, and the patience of God, who gave the world time to turn from their sins. Finally, as God promised, judgment fell! The rain came in torrents and lifted the ark, while the unbelieving world perished in the floodwaters. Only Noah and his family escaped the wrath of God.

At the end of the session, the Bisorios were in a very somber mood. They began to disband, some talking together, others reflecting quietly on the teaching. George and Bob were picking up their props when they noticed one of the Bisorio men lingering as the crowd dispersed. It was Yanou, one of their leaders, and he seemed very agitated.

"Yanou," George said, "What are you thinking about?"

"I think I'm beginning to see things more clearly," he replied.

"What are you seeing?" George queried.

"I see that you and Bob are like Noah. You have brought a message from God. But we Bisorios are like the people outside the ark, aren't we? We are worthy of God's judgment!"

"Listen Yanou!" Bob responded, "You are seeing it right. But, don't forget that God is a God of mercy. He wants to pluck off your sin and throw it away... and He will remember it no more! If you keep coming to the teaching, you will soon hear of His amazing way of escape. Promise me you won't let anything keep you from hearing God's Talk."

"I will be at every session!" The Bisorio said eagerly, "But tell me this one thing; does God's way of escape have to do with this Promised Deliverer?"

"Yes, Yanou. And soon, we will teach about Him!"

Yanou nodded his head. "I can't wait!"

Week after week, Old Testament stories were faithfully recounted. The Bisorios heard for the first time of Abraham and his acceptance by God because of his faith. They learned of "substitution," as God provided a ram to be a "sesa" for Isaac. As the teaching progressed, the crowd grew. Some of those who had feared the white skins plucked up their courage and came to hear this new "talk." 50; 60; 70 people now sat, riveted by this radical, biblical drama; a drama in which they found themselves!

The missionaries recounted Abraham's inter-cession for the city of Sodom: "'May the Lord not be angry, but let me speak just once more. What if only ten righteous people can be found in Sodom?' (Abraham asked) The Lord answered, 'If I find only ten righteous people there, then, for their sake, I will not destroy it.'" (Genesis 18: 32)

"Hear us, friends!" George called out to the people, "God could not find even ten good people in that whole city! Lot was the only one, and God took him and his daughters out of there before He poured fire and brimstone on that wicked place!" Once again, God's judgment of sin was clearly portrayed. Bob and George spared no detail in describing the immorality and perversity of Sodom; for having lived among the Bisorios for three years, the missionaries knew that these very sins were rampant in their culture!

That evening, George responded to a knock at his door. Several of the village leaders stood out-side with their string bags full of supplies. "We came to say goodbye," said Louwa. "We're leaving the village!"

"What do you mean you're leaving?'" asked George. His mind raced; why would they leave right in the middle of the teaching?

"Look at what happened to Adam and Eve when they sinned." Louwa responded. "Look at what happened to the people of Noah's time! Now you've told us of the awful judgment of Sodom and Gomorrah...look what happened to them! We are no different than those people! George, we've got to leave because, WE'RE NEXT!!"

George could tell that they were dead serious! Their own sin and God's judgment of sin was truly gripping their hearts. He coaxed the men into his home and tried to reassure them: "Please don't leave," George pleaded, "God won't send judgment on your village, because He has brought us missionaries here with the message of *mercy!* If Bob and I knew that judgment was going to fall on Basababi, do you think *we* would stay? Of course not! But we *are* staying so we can give you the heart of this message!"

After a bit more encouragement, the men agreed to stay in Basababi for the full "story." When they departed, George reflected, "Wouldn't it be something if American Christians were as conscious of God's hatred of sin as these guys are?"

In the coming weeks they learned of Israel in Egypt and of their deliverance through Moses. Bob and George took great pains to make sure the Bisorios saw the significance of the blood of the

Passover lamb. When God, "saw the blood," the angel of death passed over that household.

The Bisorios were so taken with the messages, that they often "entered into" the teaching in their hearts, feeling as if they were really "there!" As the teachers told the story of Mt. Sinai and the giving of the Ten Commandments, the villagers were caught up in the drama of Moses' trek up the mountain, and God's holy restriction, forbidding anyone to get too close, lest they die. The Bisorios "heard" the rumbling of the thunder on the mount; they "saw" the smoke and fire as the Lord descended upon His "Holy Hill!" And, they trembled, along with the children of Israel; sensing God's awesome holiness and purity:

"Woho, Awaso!" they cried, "Gode adai wede hailanege hanege sebeye. Madaga fobenaeyo!"...."Wow! No way! God is the absolute essence of all goodness! You can't even get close to Him!"

After the teaching on the Ten Commandments, many of the Bisorios were nearly in despair. The reality of their guilt before this holy God settled upon their hearts like a cloud! They had hoped that the missionaries were going to give them a list of "good works" so that they could appease God. Instead, they heard of this impossible standard that left them guilty and helpless to save themselves! The commandments did their convicting work as each Bisorio pondered his sin.

Maile sat alone in his little hut recalling all the times he had stolen food from the missionaries.

Yanou and Hadebaiyo remembered their murderous desires toward each other.

Many of the villagers realized with regret, "I've broken all ten of them! Even if I could keep all the commandments now, I could never pay for the sins of our past. But how can we keep them when God sees not only our actions, but our hearts?"

"I'm supposed to put God first...before *everything!* I've *never done that!* I always put *me* first!"

"I'm supposed to give honor to my parents. In my heart, I ridicule them."

"I'm not supposed to steal. If the missionaries knew how much of their canned food I stole when I carried it to their homes, they would never trust me again!"

"I've murdered people in my heart. I've desired other men's food, women, and weapons. I've lied and deceived."

Many of the Bisorio men and women found themselves filled with these guilty thoughts. The Law of God was leaving them without any excuses.

(13)

The Promised Deliverer

(April, 1982)

For twenty weeks the missionaries taught from the Old Testament, five days a week, nearly two hours a day. Now it was time to introduce Jesus, the Promised Deliverer.

There was an incredible expectancy among the Bisorios. The audience, which had started at 35, had now swelled to 100 people; all of them anxious to hear the "heart" of the story. Louwa, one of the village elders, along with some of the other Bisorio men, approached Bob and George before the morning's teaching:

"We are here representing our people and we have made a decision," he told the missionaries, "Not only will you teach us in the morning, you'll teach us in the evening as well!"

This "command" took the white skins completely by surprise! Teaching twice a day? They were already having trouble preparing their lessons as it was. George and Bob stepped aside and talked together. As they conferred with one another, a doubt that had been growing in their hearts surfaced. They decided to risk a confrontation with their "students:"

"Why are you coming to us and asking us to teach more often? Are you thinking that if you believe this message you'll suddenly get rich? Do you think you'll start getting more clothes or boats with outboard motors? Well listen and listen well: after we give you the heart of God's talk, you will *still* get sick; you will *still* have to go to the swamps in search of sago...and you're not getting any "cargo" (see appendix F) to make your lives easier. That's not what this message is all about!"

Louwa was unmoved by this bold challenge to their motives. He looked at the hone resolutely: "Do you really think that's all we want? If we want more clothes or goods we will work for them. That's not why we want you to teach more often. We want to hear the message because one question is burning in our chests—*we want to know what God has done about our sins!!"*

His straightforward answer completely silenced the white skins! Yet, that is exactly what they had hoped to hear. All the weeks and months of teaching were truly preparing the hearts of the Bisorios. They knew they were infected with the "sickness" of sin. It was time to introduce the "Great Physician."

The teaching about Jesus Christ completely bowled over the Bisorios! They saw that the Lord who was holding them accountable for their sins was the very One who was coming to their rescue! His miraculous conception and birth were sheer beauty to them. The missionaries had taught on the prophecy in Genesis (Gen. 3:15), which declared that the "seed of the woman" would "bruise the serpent's head." The virgin birth of Christ was unquestionably the fulfillment of that prophecy; Christ was the "seed of the woman!" (How he would "bruise the serpent's head" remained to be seen!)

The more they heard of Jesus, the more they fell in love with Him! They understood His Deity. But they loved His humanity. He walked through life and became hungry, thirsty and tired. As a carpenter, He worked with His hands.

After one of the sessions in which the missionaries had spent the whole lesson teaching on Christ's humanity, Yanou walked over to George and grinned:

"I'm so glad to hear all this about the Promised Deliverer. Now I know that He understands me! After all, what do you and Bob know? All you do is sit in your offices and study!"

When the Americans acted out Christ's temptation by the Devil in the wilderness, the villagers were captivated. They sensed the importance of the drama as Jesus was confronted by the Tempter:

"Don't give in to him!" they called from the sidelines as Satan offered his bait, "Don't listen to the liar!" Then as the Lord repelled the Enemy again and again, they clapped and cheered;

"Yes! Yes! He's resisting that old serpent! O, why couldn't *He* have been in the Garden of Eden?"

As the missionaries told story after story of Jesus, the Bisorios were blown away by His goodness and power. He healed the blind, the deaf, the crippled and the demon possessed. He could even calm storms with a mighty word of command! Jesus Christ was sweeping them off their feet. They began to refer to the Lord as, "Wede hailanege"... "the essence of goodness!"

As the days progressed in the teaching of Christ, the villagers actually made up little songs about Jesus! He was becoming their hero, and when they heard of his feeding 5,000 people with just a "lunch," they turned it into a song! When they witnessed his power in raising Lazarus from the dead, they sang about it. But not everyone sang. After hearing of the raising of Lazarus, Mawiba came up to George and Bob with tears in his eyes and said, "Jesus is the essence of goodness. Why, if He were here, He could raise my mother from the dead and she could hear God's Talk too."

The missionaries not only told of Christ's miracles, they also taught the "hard" lessons that Jesus shared. The story of the rich man who died and went to hell was incredibly gripping to the Bisorios. They saw that God was no respecter of persons and that wealth was not going to help anyone in their relationship to God. Through that story, Bob and George made it clear that there was no way you could "pay off" God and somehow "buy" forgiveness of sins. This was absolutely contrary to the Bisorio culture. Appeasing and bribing the spirits was a way of life for them. They were stunned by the realization that the Lord could *not* be bargained with. There was nothing they could do to earn His favor. "I'm not only a sinner," thought Maile. "I'm a sinner with no power to help myself. How will I ever get rid of my sins?"

Yet, somehow they knew that their eternal happiness was wrapped up in this amazing Jesus; the Promised Deliverer.

During this time of learning about the Lord Jesus, many of the Bisorios were gaining a wonderful, new knowledge . . . literacy! The painstaking process of language acquisition and creating a Bisorio alphabet was bearing fruit, not just in the Bible lessons. For now, the missionaries were able to teach the people how to read and write their own language. This was a difficult but joyful job for Noby and Harriett. They loved to see the progress in their "students."

One day, after a morning lesson about the Promised Deliverer, Harriett happened to look over Maile's shoulder as he was practicing his printing. She smiled as she read on Maile's paper, in his own words: "I really love Jesus."

He Has Put the Bow!

(May, 1982)

The Bisorios had been overwhelmed by God's creation, and now, they were captivated by Jesus Christ; God come in the flesh. There was spiritual electricity in the air! Everyone in the village sensed it.

Maile tossed and turned on his mat. George and Bob had said that the main point of God's talk would be revealed tomorrow. If only tomorrow would get here!

"Now I know why the taro lives! It is God's life, God's power that gives life to everything. He is the Creator." Maile's thoughts whirled.

But there was more, much more in his heart. For he had seen what this Mighty Creator had done to those who had rejected Him. Maile's thoughts were taken, not only by God's creation, but also by His judgment.

"I'm guilty before God; I'm sure to be judged just like the people of Noah's day. I'm just like the people of Sodom. I'm a thief. I've murdered people in my heart. God sees the sin in my heart."

Only a few moons ago, Maile had overheard the missionaries challenging the leaders of the village: "Why are you listening so attentively?" The white skins asked. "Do you think that if you believe this message you will suddenly get more clothes, or boats or outboard motors? Listen, that's not the heart of this message."

Louwa's answer to the missionaries still rang in Maile's memory: "We are listening to this message because one question is burning in our chests: *We want to know what God has done about our sins!"*

As he lay awake remembering Louwa's words, Maile softly cried from his mat, "God, O God! What have You done about <u>my</u> sins?" He knew he could not face His Creator carrying his load of sin. The thought of death now terrified Maile, for he knew of the awful place awaiting sinners. But he also understood that he could do nothing to pay for his sins himself. Maile, now only sixteen years old was wrestling with the ultimate eternal question…how can a sinful man enter the Presence of a Holy God?

Struggling with the guilt of his sin, exhaustion overtook him, and he dropped off to a fitful sleep a few hours before dawn.

The chugging of the missionaries' generator announced the morning. Though it was still dark at 5:30 am, everyone in the village came alive! This was the day when they heard the climax of the story. The light, drizzling rain didn't dampen their spirits at all! Before it was even light, the Bisorios, now over 100 in number, headed up the hill to the meeting place.

As they prepared the props for the reenactment of the story, Bob and George were excited too. They had been up till 3:00 am praying fervently about this day. For three and a half years, all their language and culture study; all their bouts with malaria; all their discouragements; every waking moment of their lives had led up to this! "Well, my brother," said Bob, as he looked at the life-size cross they had made, "Today is the day!"

"Do you think anyone will believe?" George asked. "After all this, what if no one believes God's Good News?"

"We've just got to be faithful to proclaim the Truth," Bob replied. "Then the results are up to God."

They suddenly noticed that the bustle in the village had ceased. Where there had been noise and activity, now there was a strange quiet. Was this a last minute lack of interest? Had everyone gone back to bed? Then they heard a knock at their door.

"Hey, where are you guys?" said a voice outside the door. "We want to hear the end of the story! Have you gone back to sleep?"

Back to sleep! The white skins shook their heads and laughed. "We're coming!" they called. Then they grabbed all the props and materials and hurried up the hill.

As they approached the top, a group of Bisorios jumped up and pointed to the sky; "Oi dae, oi dae! Lomo eyamo, lomo eyamo!"... "Look, look!" they cried, "He's put the bow! He's put the bow!"

The missionaries looked heavenward and their hearts leapt! The parting clouds and mists revealed a flawless, shimmering rainbow arching across the sky!

Louwa stood and waved his finger at his countrymen. "God has set His bow in the sky to tell us that we need to listen to this message. He wants our undivided attention!"

So, after God got everyone's attention, the teaching began! To the Bisorios, everything they had heard about Jesus Christ was brand new. Over the last few weeks, He had become their hero; the One who healed the sick, and fed the hungry. When they heard that He resisted the devil in the wilderness, they exclaimed, "O, why couldn't Jesus have been the One in the Garden of Eden!"

This incredible Lord Jesus: He calmed the storm with just a word; He gave sight to the blind. Yet, he became weary, hungry and thirsty. He was truly man and truly God!

But this day, something was wrong with the message. Jesus had been arrested and was being tried for crimes He had not committed!

As the missionaries acted out Christ's trial before Pontius Pilate, the Bisorios were outraged. When Pilate offered to release Him, some of them stood up and shouted, "Let Him go! Yeah, let Him go!" They were so agitated, that Bob and George had to move them back to their "seats" telling them that was not how the story went!

"Why doesn't Jesus do something?" Maile wondered as he watched the drama. "He could kill them all with a wave of His hand. Why doesn't He defend Himself?" He watched in horror as Christ was flogged and then led off to be nailed to a cross. Since the Bisorios had never heard of crucifixion, the missionaries reenacted Christ's death. Bob, playing the part of Jesus, hung there on the cross, with mock blood dripping from his wounds. From his vantage point, Bob could see the agony of the Bisorio people. Men were rocking back and forth in despair. Women clutched each other and wept. It couldn't be! The Promised Deliverer was being killed before their eyes.

Yet they all gazed at the cross, watching through their tears in stunned silence. Then they flinched in sympathetic pain as the soldier thrust his spear into Jesus' side. The gushing blood told them that the unthinkable had happened. He was dead. Their hero was dead. They were overwhelmed at seeing his now lifeless body.

Since the story of Jesus was brand new to them, the Bisorios got to experience some of the grief that Christ's followers felt when He was put into the tomb. But George and Bob didn't want to make them wait three days! So they quickly acted out the resurrection of Christ. The Son of God was alive again and their grief quickly turned to joy. Two other missionaries, Jack Housley and Rich Prohaska played the parts of Roman soldiers who fell down as dead men when Christ arose.

The white skins then taught about the Risen Lord and His visits with his disciples. Finally they spoke of the commission He had given His followers, telling them to go into the world to preach the Good News.

The Bisorios sat, totally engrossed in the teaching. They were overjoyed that Christ had risen, but....

"Why did Jesus have to die?" Maile wondered. "He is the promised Deliverer, so why did He allow Himself to be killed? There has to be more to the story."

(15)

The Lamb of God
(May, 1982)

The Bisorios were on pins and needles; they all shared Maile's question: What is the rest of the story? As Bob and George prepared to wrap up the teaching, their wives and the other four missionaries who were there quietly prayed, "Father, reveal Your truth to our friends."

George was busting at the seams; "You are about to hear the rest of the story!" he shouted to the crowd. "Jesus sent his followers into the world to share this news, and now His message is coming to **you!** The question is, will you believe it?"

Bob continued, "Do you remember Abel's sacrifice? It was a blood sacrifice and God accepted it. Now you have heard of Christ's blood sacrifice. Listen! Just as He accepted Abel's offering, God the Father has accepted the sacrifice of His Son...for you!"

"And what about Isaac?" George continued. "Abraham went to the mountain to sacrifice him. But did he die? No! God provided a substitute ram. The ram was slain in Isaac's place." George held out his hands pleading with the Bisorios. "Don't you see? Just like that ram, Jesus had been slain for you. He is your "sesa," your substitute. You should have died for your own sins, but Jesus took your place!"

As they recounted the Bible stories that they had taught for five straight months, the missionaries saw the lights beginning to come on, "click, click, click" in the eyes of their friends. They were "connecting the dots!" All the Old Testament sacrifices were foreshadowing the true sacrifice; Jesus, the Lamb of God!

Excitedly, Bob and George took turns teaching, speaking of the Passover Lamb and the serpent being raised in the wilderness. A murmur began to rise from the crowd.

Finally, Bob spoke of Noah: "Because Noah believed God, he entered the ark and was saved from God's righteous judgment. Jesus is our 'ark of safety!' If we believe in Jesus, our sins will be forgiven, and we too will be saved from the wrath of God."

Bob was in mid-sentence when the oldest man in the village started waving his hand; "Bob, Bob!" he cried, "I need to say something!"

"Yes, Wakeya," said a startled Bob as he turned to this frail man, hunched on the ground. "What is it you want to say?"

"Bob, are you saying that all I have to do is *believe* that Jesus died for me, and God will forgive my sins?"

Yes, Wakeya," smiled Bob, "That's *exactly* what I'm saying!"

"O, Bob," he exclaimed with tears welling up in his eyes, "I *do* believe! I *do* believe! Help me up, quickly!"

Bob pulled Wakeya to his feet and placed his hands on the old man's shoulders. As he looked up into the missionary's face, a tearful Wakeya burst into testimony: "I believe that Jesus died on the cross for me! It should have been me on that cross; I'm the guilty one. But God loved me and sent His Son to die in my place. I give Him my heart!"

Now the murmur was swelling, as Bisorios spoke back and forth to each other. The truth was sinking in. Hameyagu was pacing across the back of the meeting place. George called out to him, "Hameyagu! Do you want to say something?

Hameyagu, dressed only in his grass "skirt" and a baseball cap given him by the missionaries, walked over and stood on a stump. "I believe that when Jesus shed His blood, He shed it for me! And when He died, He died for me." His face became radiant as his voice grew louder, "And if Jesus would not have died for me, I would have died in my sins and gone to hell!"

George and Bob were blown away! They were astonished to hear such a clear testimony of faith! "We've got to respond to that!" George exclaimed to Bob.

"Well, go ahead," Bob said, "Say something!"

"Hameyagu!" George called, "If you really do believe in Jesus, then on the authority of the Word of God, I tell you that God has plucked off all of your sins; He has thrown them away; And now, it is just as if you never committed them; they will be remembered no more! All concerns about your sins are dead and will never be mentioned again! Jesus paid for your sins and purchased eternal life for you!"

Still standing on the stump, Hameyagu's face was glowing. "My sins are gone!" he cried as he raised his hands and broke into an ecstatic smile!

Then the murmur burst into an uproar! All over the place, Bisorios were telling one another of their faith in Christ. People were laughing; people were crying and hugging each other for joy.

Maile's mind was reeling. He was absolutely stunned! Just hours before as he lay awake, he had asked God what He had done about his sins. Now, here was the answer; totally unexpected; totally overwhelming: God *Himself,* had died for Maile's sins! He found himself on his feet and began to wander down the hill, oblivious to the excited chatter of his countrymen. His heart was overwhelmed as the truth of God's love crashed upon him again and again…. "He did it for me, for me, for me!"

The missionaries noticed Maile walking away. "Hey Maile," Bob called, "where are you going?" To Bob's utter surprise, the Bisorio teenager ignored him! In the midst of all the rejoicing, Maile looked sober, even sad. And the white skins wondered what he was going on in his mind.

Maile staggered down to his hut. He needed to get away from the crowd and just think...think about Promised Deliverer; the Lamb of God!

Meanwhile, the Bisorio ladies were crowding around Noby and Harriett, crying for joy, and thanking them for coming to tell them about Jesus.

"Don't thank us," Harriett exclaimed through her tears of joy, "We're just messengers..."

"That's right," laughed Doneyaka, "We shouldn't thank you...Jesus is the One Who died for us!"

A spirit of rejoicing came upon this meeting place in the jungles of Papua New Guinea. Of the 100 people who heard the message, at least 80 of them were now new believers in Christ! Many of them spoke together of God's wonderful forgiveness. Some of them, like Maile, went to their homes to be alone with their Savior. All of them were transported into the "joy of salvation."

The four missionary couples were blown away and emotionally drained. After an hour of hearing testimony after testimony, they walked down to the Kennell's house to "catch their breath!" As they passed the door of Salugu's home, they heard his voice, almost as if he were singing a song. So, they glanced in the hut and saw him, lying on his back with his bent knees pumping up and down. As the soles of his feet slapped out the rhythm and his body rocked from side to side, he chanted, "My Jesus, what have You done for me? My Jesus, what have You done for me? Jesus, Jesus, what have You done for me?" The thrill and emotional release of being forgiven by the Lord of the universe seemed to charge the atmosphere of the village with rapture. Salugu's song captured that universal joy: "My Jesus, what have you done for me?"

That evening, the Bisorios gathered again, around the cross that was still standing at the top of the hill. Each of them had a unique story of how God had touched them. Bob and George met with them, one on one, encouraging them and asking them to express the reason for their joy.

As they talked together at the meeting place, Maile emerged from his hut and walked up the hill. His face was still sober. Bob rose to greet the young man and put his arm around his shoulder. "Well Maile," he said, "What do you think?"

Maile looked thoughtfully at his friend.

"Bob, as you shared God's Talk with us, I came to understand that I was filled with sin and could not save myself from God's wrath. Louwa's question kept haunting me; 'What has God done about our sins?' Then today I heard that Jesus died for me, and it was more than I could take in! I had to go and be alone.

"But now I have come up to tell you that I believe in the Lord Jesus Christ! Because He spilled His blood for me, my sins are forgiven. And now, I no longer belong to myself, I belong to Him!"

Now Maile's sober face changed and became a picture of beaming joy; "Yes, Bob, my sins are forgiven! God has made me His own possession...not just for this life, but for all eternity!"

Bob and Maile threw their arms around each other and laughed and cried in sheer delight. This white-skin from California and this teenage villager from Papua New Guinea were now brothers in the family of God.

When the missionaries finally left the meeting hill that evening, the villagers were still talking, laughing and praying together in utter bliss. Every few minutes, a new group of Bisorio men would prance, arm in arm around the cross and sing spontaneous songs about Jesus, their Promised Deliverer. Their joyful celebration lasted far into the night.

Late that night, as an exhausted, but joyful George Walker lay in bed, a verse of scripture came into his heart:

"...Jesus, full of joy through the Holy Spirit, said, 'I praise you, Father, Lord of heaven and earth, because you have hidden these things from the wise and learned, and revealed them to little children. Yes, Father, for this was your good pleasure.'" *(Luke 10:21)*

In this isolated, forgotten corner of the world, Almighty God, by His good pleasure and amazing mercy, revealed Himself to the Bisorio people.

The Power of the Gospel

(August 1982)

Three months after the glorious "day of salvation," Harriett Walker had no fears of being alone in the village of Basababi. Nearly all of her Bisorio friends were now Christians and were showing amazing changes in their lives. Most of them were reading and writing in their own language, and they studied their Bible lessons diligently. As newborn babes in Christ, they were learning the incredible joy of prayer...talking to their Heavenly Father. Marital strife had all but disappeared, even in Kabalame's hut! This man who had nearly speared his wife a few years prior was quickly being recognized as a changed man... a "man of peace!"

So, Harriett felt no fear when her husband, George took off for a few days up the river to assist some other missionaries in a different tribe. Even though the Bob and Noby Kennell were away too, she felt safe surrounded by her Bisorio brothers and sisters.

Her four and a half year old son, Georgie awoke that morning with a fever. Harriett noticed other symptoms that indicated malaria, so she administered the usual medication to her boy. The little guy quickly fell asleep on their couch. A couple of hours later, Harriett called, "Hey Georgie! Time to get up." There was no response.

Harriett came out of her kitchen and tried to awaken him. He was burning with fever, and seemed almost comatose. She shook him and talked to him; she put cool, wet cloths on his face, but he did not come to consciousness.

She had treated hundreds of cases of malaria in the village and she knew the medical routine. But this was Harriett's only son. She looked down upon her feverish little body and found a helpless despair welling up within her heart...She panicked!

Harriett grabbed the radio and began calling everyone she could think of. But no one answered! She tried to reach the mission station where George had gone...no response. She remembered a husband / wife medical team who *always* manned their radio for emergencies... there was silence on the other end! Frantically Harriett kept calling into the silence.

Just then, Doneyaka looked into Harriett's home. She instantly saw the fear on Harriett's face. "Hawiyede, hanege biyame" ("Harriet, what's wrong?")

"O, Doneyaka," she said as she burst into tears. "It's Georgie. He's so sick and I don't know what to do. I've tried to call a doctor, but he isn't answering. I wish George hadn't gone away. If only he were here…"

Doneyaka hurried into the house to try to help Harriett. A moment later, her husband, Kabalame came to the door and knocked. Harriett called for him to come in, and immediately, he was at her side looking gravely at her sick son.

"Kabalame!" Harriett wailed. "Georgie is very sick. And here I am, all alone. I've tried to call George on the radio, but I can't get a hold of him. I wish he were here. He'd know what to do…" Harriett began to sob and tell Kabalame and Doneyaka all that had happened and all she had tried to do for her son. She kept repeating her wish that her husband could be there to help her and take care of little Georgie. They tried to calm her down, but she was becoming more and more frantic. And the absence of George was more than she could bear as she looked help-lessly at her son.

Suddenly, Kabalame spoke; "Idose adai Godedobaba,eba?"

Harriett stopped and wiped her eyes, "What did you say, Kabalame?"

"I said, 'So George is God, is he?"

Harriett was stunned by the question.

Kabalame, looked earnestly at Harriett and, once again, repeated the question: "So George is God, is he?"

Harriett turned her tear-stained face to her Bisorio friend and shook her head: "No, Kabalame. George is not God."

Kabalame continued, "Harriett, who is the giver of life?"

Harriett looked at her brother in Christ; "God is the giver of life, Kabalame."

"That's right. Tell me Harriett. Is God good?"

"Yes, Kabalame, God is good."

"Harriett, God is good, He is the giver of life, and He is the only healer. George can't heal; doctors can't heal; medicine can't heal. God is the Healer."

This brand new believer in Christ continued; "If God chooses to let Georgie live, He is still God, and He is still good. If God chooses to let Georgie die, He is still God, and He is still good."

Harriett felt a calm come upon her. "You're right Kabalame," she stammered. "I know you're right, but, but, I just don't know what to do."

Kabalame sat down on the couch by the feverish little boy. He placed one of his strong hands on Georgie's head, and one on his shoulder. Until three months ago, the Bisorio language had never been used to pray to Almighty God, but now this Bisorio man bowed his head and began to intercede in his native tongue for Harriett's son:

"Great God; Giver of life. You have given this precious little boy to George and Harriett. He belongs to you and You can take him if you want to. But we want him to stay with us. So we are asking that You heal him of this sickness. Also, please help Harriett. Give her Your peace and the knowledge to treat him, even as she has treated so many of our people. It is Your will that we want. You are good and we trust You. And I am praying this because of Jesus, Your One and Only Son."

Harriett looked upon Kabalame with gratitude and wonder. She felt the peace of God flood her soul and then, she calmly gave Georgie his next dose of medicine.

Kabalame and Doneyaka stayed with her, watching and praying and helping her around the house. In a couple of hours, the little boy's fever broke. He began to breathe normally and opened his eyes.

The good Giver of Life graciously answered Kabalame's prayer and healed little Georgie.

When George Walker returned from his journey, he found his family healthy and happy. He also found that this new "congregation" of Christians was becoming a radical group of "prayer warriors." When they became Christians and threw out all their tormenting spirits, they realized that the Lord Jesus Christ was much more powerful than their former gods! Instead of trying to appease the spirits, they came to Christ in prayer for *everything!* They actually believed that when their sins had been for-given, they had immediate access to their Savior. And, they believed that He loved them enough to answer their heart-felt prayers!

(17)

"What's Going On Downriver?"

George chewed slowly and thoughtfully, "Well?" Mawiba asked as he watched his friend eat. "What do you think?"

George swallowed hard. He was trying to think of a diplomatic answer. "I think that grub-worms are probably really good when you get used to them!"

"Of course, they're good!" Mawiba chided, "But you didn't answer my question. Don't you think they taste like popcorn?"

"Mawiba," George responded, "You already know that my tastes and your tastes are a lot different. But if you think grubs taste like popcorn, that's great." As he looked at his friend, George was thinking "That squishy, disgusting worm tastes *nothing* like popcorn!"

Though they didn't agree on the "goodness" of grubs, they *did* agree that popcorn was great! When the missionaries introduced popcorn to the

Bisorios, they instantly loved it! So, sitting around the hone's living room, talking and munching a bowl of popcorn became a regular event in Basababi. Often, as evening was approaching, a few of the neighbors would wander over to the Walker's or the Kennell's house and hang around. So, Harriett or Noby would break out the utensils and pop up a batch of popcorn on the propane stove!

After so many of the tribe believed in Jesus, these get-togethers became even more special. For now, they were not merely friends; they were brothers and sisters in Christ, meeting to talk about their new life in Jesus!

So, Bob wasn't surprised, after a knock on his door at suppertime, to open and see four Bisorios waiting to enter. What *did* surprise him were the very serious looks on their faces. This evening, Hadebaiyo and three of his friends hadn't come over looking for popcorn; they were extremely upset and came looking for some answers!

Sensing that something was very wrong with his friends, Bob called to his wife, "Honey, go ahead and start dinner without me. I think Hadebaiyo has a problem."

The four men came in and plumped on the floor. "Hadebaiyo," Bob said, "What in the world is wrong?"

"I just need you to answer some questions for us," replied Hadebaiyo."

"Sure thing. Go ahead."

"How long have you known this Good News of salvation in Jesus?"

"I've known it all my life, Hadebaiyo."

"Did your father know this Good News?"

"Yes, my father knew it."

"Did your grandfather know it?"

"Yes, Hadebaiyo, my grandfather knew it too."

The Bisorio man thought for a moment. In his culture, there was no word for "great grandfather."

"Well," Hadebaiyo continued, "Did the generations before your grandfather know this talk about Jesus?"

Bob did his best to explain that in America, the Gospel had been known for over 200 years!

The four Bisorio men muttered among themselves for a moment, then their leader posed another question; "Bob, how long have missionaries been in Papua New Guinea?"

"I think the first missionaries came to this country about 85 years ago," Bob replied.

"And how long have there been missionaries in the Sepik region, close to our ground?"

"There have been other missionaries in this area for about 20 years."

Hadebaiyo rose to his feet and walked to the end of the room. He paused a moment at the window, then he turned and faced the missionary. There were tears in his eyes.

"Bob," he said, trying to control his sorrow, "You have answered some of our questions. But this is our main question...*What is going on downriver?* You white skins have had this Good News for generation upon generation and we are just getting it now? WHAT IS GOING ON DOWNRIVER?"

A thousand thoughts flew into Bob's mind at once! He tried to formulate an answer for his agitated friend, but Hadebaiyo's heart was overflowing;

"You have told us all along how important this message is. And now we know and believe it! But why didn't someone come to tell my mother and father before they died? They were still alive 20 seasons ago! They could have been freed from their fears. They could have had their sins forgiven and escaped the fire pit if someone would have told them the message! What is wrong with the Christians downriver?"

This was more than Bob could handle! Now, his eyes brimmed with tears as he walked over, arms outstretched to his distraught friend. The two brothers in Christ hugged and wept together.

Finally, Bob spoke; "Hadebaiyo, I have asked the same question a hundred times and I don't have a good answer to it. Something is very wrong downriver, for we surely have the resources to take this Good News everywhere. But...we don't. I can only say that, even though we are very late, George, Harriett, Noby and I *did* come!"

"And for that, I will thank God forever," replied the Bisorio amidst his tears. "But I can't shake the grief of knowing so many of my people have died without Christ."

Bob sat down with his brothers and they shared their sadness. They talked. They wept. They prayed. Finally, Hadebaiyo and his friends headed back to their own homes.

Bob watched his four brothers in Christ leave. As he remained at the door for a moment, his wife, Noby, having tucked the girls in bed, joined him. He recounted the meeting with the men. Then, gazing into the starlit night they turned their hearts heavenward:"Father," they prayed, "Why do we keep the message of salvation to ourselves when so many are dying and entering a Christ-less eternity? Please do a new work in your people. There are so many who still haven't heard Your Good News. Send forth laborers into Your harvest field.

"Our King and our God, stir up the hearts of Christians around the world. By the power of Your Spirit, broadcast Hadebaiyo's question to the ends of the earth…

…'What's going on downriver?'"

Author's Afterward

I experienced the sweet, humbling privilege of hiking into "Bisorio country" in Papua New Guinea exactly 24 years after the Bisorios received the Good News of Christ. Thanks to the tireless work of the missionaries, the Bisorio believers now have the entire New Testament and much of the Old Testament in their own language. They continue to reach out to other Bisorio hamlets, taking the Good News of Christ to their own people. It is an on-going story of salvation among the Bisorio people.

After we settled into the hut they built for us, I spent a couple of days interviewing a number of the Bisorio brothers for this book. With Bob Kennell and George Walker translating, I had a sweet time of fellowship with these amazing brothers in Christ.

Maile, now in his early forties, is a powerful preacher and evangelist, respected by all his countrymen. I'll never forget the look of joy and transport on Maile's face as we talked and he remembered that glorious day in 1982 when he was saved. As George looked at his happy brother, he decided to ask him a different question:

"Maile," he asked, "On that day, the day you received Christ; was that the day that God marked you to belong to Him?"

Maile looked at the missionary with shining eyes; "O no, George," he answered, "God marked me to belong to Him before the foundation of the world!"

There are still over 2,000 people groups in the world who do not have "God's Talk" in their language.

For more information contact:

NTM USA
1000 E. First Street Sanford, FL 32771

ntm@ntm.org

407-323-3430

George Walker
george_walker@ntm.org

Bob Kennell
bob_kennell@ntm.org

Rob Greenslade
snowygrove@gmail.com

A portion of the proceeds from this book will go to help the Bisorio people of Papua New Guinea.

Glossary

Bisorio Terms

Aiyago (ay-ah'-go): Black Magic

Balaibaga (bah-ly'-bah-gah): The Bisorio village with an airstrip

Basababi (bah-sah-bah'-bee): The Bisorio village to first welcome missionaries

Babadiyao (bah-bah-dee-yah'-o): A healing meeting with the witch doctor

Bisorio (bee-so'-dee-o) A small nation of people in Papua New Guinea

Daise (dy'-say) A bone dagger

Duga Anege (doo'-ga an'-i-gay) "Tobacco Mother," the spirit or force that empowers the witch doctor during babadiyao

Gise-Mawi (ghee'-say maow'-ee) The edible top core of the sago palm tree

Gonimai (go'-nee-my): The prince of the evil spirits

Hone (ho'-nay) white skin (singular or plural)

Sowanaga (so-wah'-ni-ka): Dead ancestor spirit

Yama (yah'-mah): Small jungle spirits, one of the killers of man

Other Terms
Downriver: Anywhere outside of Bisorio land

Waiting at the Neck: Deceitful friendship for revenge

Shaman: Witch doctor

Pidgin English: The trade language of Papua New Guinea

Bisorio Names
Bagowai (bag'-o-wi): The witch doctor

Doneyaka (doe'-nyah-kah): Bisorio woman, wife of Kabalame

Hadebaiyo (hah-di-by'-o): Bisorio leader

Hameyagu (hahm'-ee-ah-goo) Young Bisorio bachelor

Kabalame (kah'-blah-may): Bisorio man, husband of Doneyaka

Louwa (lo'-wah): Bisorio leader

Maile (my'-lay): Bisorio teenager

Mawiba (mow'-ee-bah): Bisorio language helper

Yanou (yah'-no): Bisorio leader and language helper

<u>Appendices</u>

Apendix A: Chronological Teaching

New Tribes Mission and other missions organizations have adopted a method of Bible teaching for evangelism and discipleship called, "Chronological Teaching." This means, simply, that the Bible is taught in the order in which it was revealed to man. This method of teaching begins with creation and continues historically until it culminates with the story of Christ, and the spread of the church. Thus, the Bible is seen as one, continuous story from Genesis to Revelation. It is taught in its God-given, historical and narrative context. Using this method, Bible doctrines are understood, not as isolated teachings, but as realities expressed in history. God Himself is seen as the Author and Main Character of the story, and His attributes and heart shine throughout the biblical account.

For example, after the Bisorios had been taught the book of Genesis, they were asked, "Does God hate sin?" Their answer was not based on a theological system. Instead, they answered according to the Story...they said, "Does God hate sin? Just look what He did when Adam and Eve sinned! Look what He did in Noah's day! And what about Sodom and Gomorrah?...He destroyed them for their sin. Of course God hates sin!" God's attitude toward sin was obvious, portrayed as it was in the framework of His Word.

Another important feature of "Chronological Teaching" is that the worldview of the Bible is always at the forefront. As the narrative unfolds, God's viewpoint is clearly seen. And, as His viewpoint is held in contrast to other beliefs, it soon becomes apparent that the Lord's worldview is in direct opposition to all other philosophies. By the time the Bisorios were presented with the Gospel, they clearly understood that to embrace Jesus was to throw away, not just their sin, but their false worldview as well. Thus, there was much less danger of "syncretism," the mixing of religious systems together.

Appendix B: Bisorio Conversations

As the missionaries were learning the language of the people, many conversations were going on right under their noses that they could not understand! The Bisorios bantered back and forth with one another, talking about the white skins. Often, everyone in the village would be talking about the same issue concerning the "hone."

Later, when the Bisorios became Christians, they told the missionaries the things they had said about them years before:

"Everyone was wondering if you were sowanaga, departed ancestor spirits!"

"We thought you would bring a curse upon our gardens."

"We were all afraid that you would steal our children or our wives!"

"We thought that you would share your cargo. Then, after a time of waiting, we thought, 'Why don't we just kill them and take all their cargo?'"

"We saw you trying so hard to learn our language, and knew that you loved us!"

"We could tell that the white skin men truly loved their wives!"

"We all knew you were happy because of God's Talk."

The universal testimony of the Bisorios is; "everyone in the village was talking about these things." The village was alive with these conversations, but the missionaries were unaware. Since these discussions happened years earlier, and there is no memory of the specific dialogs, the author has taken the liberty of reconstructing a few key conversations to facilitate the flow of the story.

Appendix C: Tribal Court System

As the Bisorios moved from small, family hamlets into larger village settings, they developed a workable system for solving disputes among the tribe. Woven deeply into the Bisorio culture is a strong sense of justice; the belief that every wrong deserves some kind of recompense. Though they did not have the books of Moses, (prior to the arrival of the missionaries) they clearly understood the principle of, "an eye for an eye."

In the Bisorio society, disputes could arise in every imaginable relationship. Since the raising of pigs and the cultivation of gardens is a part of every Bisorio's life, disputes often arose concerning these issues. For example, a pig belonging to one family might break out of its pen and get into a neighbor's garden and root it up. One pig can wreck a garden overnight! And this is a huge offense, for the garden is the main food source for the Bisorios.

The "court" would be a meeting between the two families. They would sit in a circle in an appointed place with an "arbitrator" standing in the middle. Acting as the judge and lawyer for both sides, his job was to "straighten the talk." He would listen to the "talk" from all the family members, ask questions, clarify statements, etc. He was chosen for his ability to think and speak with wisdom and impartiality. In the case of the Bisorios, Hadebaiyo was usually the arbitrator because he had keen insight and an unusual grasp of language and communication. His job was to finally arrive at an amount of restitution that was fair to both families.

Depending upon the severity of the offense, the "court" could take a couple of hours, or a couple of days! Because of the community bond of the tribe, and the need for village harmony, this system of justice worked surprisingly well.

Appendix D: Language Consultation

New Tribes Mission is committed to the principle that the Gospel of Jesus Christ is best understood and received in the "heart language" of any people group. There are many sad examples worldwide of language groups who have supposedly "heard the Gospel," when if fact, they have only picked up bits and pieces of Christianity through a trade language that they barely understand. This usually results in "syncretism," where people will add a little bit of Jesus to their false religion and think that they are saved.

It is critical that the missionaries gain a good understanding of the language and the culture in which they are working. This is of course important for interpersonal communication. But, it is vital when the Bible is being translated into the peoples' tongue.

As tribal missionaries are learning the language and culture of the people, they are checked periodically by language consultants who ascertain their progress. This process involves grammatical and linguistic testing in both oral and written language acquisition.

The process is especially difficult with a language, like Bisorio, which is unknown and unwritten. The following example is very simplified, but it should give the reader an idea of how the consultant can determine a missionary's proficiency:

The consultant will meet with the missionary and one of his tribal language helpers. This language helper must be somewhat fluent in the trade language. Then, there can be a three-way connection in this meeting based on three languages: English connects the consultant to the missionary; Pidgin, (the trade language) connects the consultant to the tribal person; Bisorio (in this case) connects the tribal person to the missionary.

The consultant will talk privately to the language helper in the Pidgin language. He will say something like, "Speak to the missionary in the Bisorio tongue and tell him, 'I think it is going to rain tonight.'" The language helper will then repeat the sentence to the missionary in the Bisorio language. Finally, the missionary will repeat the sentence back to the consultant in English. If the sentence that the missionary repeats is the same as the one given by the consultant to the language helper, all is well. If there is a big discrepancy, then the missionary needs more work in the Bisorio tongue.

New Tribes and other "front line" missions have developed amazing accuracy in the science of language consultation. This is because of their unwavering commitment to see the Gospel of Jesus Christ proclaimed to "every tribe and tongue and people and nation." (Revelation 5:9, 7:9, 14:6)

Appendix E: Animism

The predominant worldview among tribal people is called Animism. This was the worldview of the Bisorios prior to embracing Jesus Christ and a biblical life philosophy.

The Worldview Resource Group has said that Animism is, "A worldview that understands human existence to be environed by numerous and diverse spirit beings and impersonal forces that affect human experience and well-being. It is held within this system that man can control or significantly influence these capricious entities by proper incantations, rituals, offerings, sacrifices, or magic to bring about desired outcomes."

The Bisorios believed their world was inhabited by spirit beings who controlled nearly every aspect of life. It was thought by the tribe that if they could appease and manipulate the spirits, all would go well for them; their gardens would produce, the hunt would be successful, they would enjoy good health, etc. On the other hand, if something went wrong, it was generally believed that one of the spirits was displeased. The missionaries regularly witnessed the sacrificing of pigs to the "sowanaga," the spirits of dead ancestors. This was often done when someone became ill, to determine which spirit was angry and then, to attempt to appease him.

In his study of Animism, George Walker has said, "Animists, like most adherents of non-Western religions, have a *holistic* view of life. In having a holistic perspective, the animist sees himself totally surrounded by a dynamic, unpredictable and interconnected world of humans, animals, plants, spirit beings, gods, goddesses, ancestors, and magic."

It was vitally important that the Kennells and the Walkers understood this spirit world before they began teaching the Bible's viewpoint to the Bisorio people.

Appendix F: Cargo Cult

There is widespread belief among the animistic tribal people of Papua New Guinea that the amazing wealth of industrialized societies can be obtained through spiritual means.

This view was fostered during World War II, when Papua New Guinea (PNG) became a base of operations for the Japanese and then the allies. The technology, munitions, planes, ships, clothing, tools and food that was landed upon PNG was mind-boggling to these isolated tribal people. Because of their worldview and their lack of exposure to industry, they assumed that all this wealth was given to the soldiers do to the "rituals" they performed.

After the war, some of the people of PNG, hoping to bring back the "cargo" that had inundated their land, began copying the Japanese and the allies. "Cargo Cult" is the belief that by performing the practices of the rich society, the spirits will bestow the wealth, or "cargo" to the one doing the rituals.

The missionaries wanted to be certain that the Bisorios' excitement to hear "God's Talk" was not based on this false expectation. They did not want their Bisorio friends to think that by adopting the "religion" of the missionaries that they would magically receive clothes, food, tools, etc.

Appendix G: The "Unbiased" Documentary

(Editor's note: This event takes place in 1988, about six years after the Good News of Christ had been given to the Bisorios. An airstrip has been built a few miles from the original village, so the missionaries and all of the people have relocated to be near the airstrip. This new village is called Balaibaga. Due to health problems, the Kennells are not living there, but have moved to the mission headquarters in the town of Garoka. Another couple, Bob and Sue Parry have moved in to assist the Walkers.

We have included this episode to confront a deep-seated opinion that nations which have never heard of Christ, should be "left alone." This opinion states that these non-Christian societies are "happier" in their traditional beliefs, and should not be bothered by Christians. The following story will show, by the Bisorios' own testimony that they were miserable in their traditional beliefs, and they are overjoyed that the missionaries brought them the truth.

Because of the sensitive nature of this chapter, we have changed the names of the broadcasting company and crew. But this event really took place, and is written as recounted by the missionaries and the Bisorio people.)

The village was alive with curiosity as the Impartial Broadcasting Company team unloaded their equipment from the missions airplane: Cameras, boom microphones, recording equipment. The crew consisted of six support personnel and a male and female reporter.

"Welcome to the village of Balaibaga," smiled George Walker as he held out his hand to the head reporter. She shook his hand graciously.

"Thank you. I'm Shirley Irewood and this is my associate, Richard Britland." She smiled a professional smile, and then began to direct the camera team as George talked to Mr. Britland. After all the gear was unloaded, the missionaries led the production crew to the Walker's house. Miss Irewood, paused for a moment outside the house.

"I notice your home is quite a bit larger than the Bisorio's huts."

"Well, yes," George replied, "We haven't entirely adopted the same lifestyle as the Bisorios."

"I see," she replied shortly.

Once inside, the two reporters outlined their plan for the next couple of days. They hoped to do a documentary on modern missions.

"Our goal," said Mr. Britland, "is to try to portray the daily life of modern-day missionaries. We will be visiting other missions stations as well, but yours was highly recommended by your headquarters in Sanford, Florida. We are thinking about calling the story 'Onward Christian Soldiers.'" The Walkers expressed their delight that they could host the reporters.

"Whatever we can do to make your stay comfortable and productive, please let us know," said Harriett.

After some iced tea and a short visit, the broadcasting team was taken to their host homes. They planned to be up early to begin shooting.

The next three days were pretty grueling for the missionaries. The reporters wanted to know their daily routine and filmed nearly every aspect of their life. They filmed George and Bob Kennell (who had flown in to help with the interviews) on their morning jog up and down the airstrip. They filmed Harriett and Sue as they worked around the house. They seemed especially interested in the few modern conveniences belonging to the Walkers and Parrys.

"I don't suppose the villagers have any of these...." Miss Irewood was pointing to Harriett's blender.

"It would be difficult for them to use one without a generator," replied Harriett. "And to be honest," continued Harriet, "we hardly ever use it ourselves because firing up the generator is a hassle." The reporter paused a moment, looking at the blender. Then she noticed the intercom.

"This seems rather, mmmm...extravagant in this setting," she noted.

"Well, it's extremely handy when we need to communicate with the Parrys in their house," replied Harriet.

"Oh, I'm sure it is handy, indeed," cooed Miss Irewood, with a smile.

As the days with the broadcasting company wore on, it became evident that they were more interested in the lifestyle of the missionaries than the changed lives of the Bisorio believers. Teaching from the Bible had now been a part of the Bisorio's lives for six years. For them, it was the highlight of the day as they learned more about Jesus who loved them and had forgiven them. But, when the time for teaching and testimonies came around, the IBC people packed up their cameras and called it a day. They didn't record any footage of these joyful Christians proclaiming their newfound faith and rejoicing in the freedom of being forgiven.

The night before the IBC was scheduled to leave, Miss Irewood asked to meet with a few of the Bisorio men. "I'd like to get 'up close and personal' to find out just how their lives have changed since you have lived among them," she said.

"Finally," George thought, "Maybe now they will understand why we came here." So, he invited four of the men into his house and they all sat around the living room together—George, Bob, the Bisorio men, and the two reporters.

George translated back and forth as Miss Irewood asked questions and the men answered. She wanted to know if they were happy that the missionaries had come. The four men nodded their heads enthusiastically and smiled. "Our children are much healthier," commented Kabene. "We are too!" Laughed Maile, and they all chuckled. "Everyone called us 'wild animals,'" Said Odeya. "Neighboring tribes told the missionaries to leave those 'jungle pigs' alone. But they came anyway. Yes, we are healthier, but the best thing is that Bob and Noby, George and Harriett brought us the good news of Jesus."

George smiled to hear the sincere responses these guys gave to the reporter. But, he noticed that Miss Irewood was not writing anything in her notepad.

After listening to them for a few minutes, she cocked her head to one side and asked very sweetly, "What things have changed since the missionaries came that you *really miss* and wish that you could go back to?"

George translated the question to the men; then there was a long silence. The four Bisorios glanced back and forth at each other with puzzled looks. They furrowed their brows and quietly spoke to one another, trying to make sense of her question.

Then Mawiba, one of the language helpers, turned his gaze upon Miss Irewood. It dawned on him that she actually believed that they had been happier before the missionaries came! He smiled knowingly at her, shaking his head. The Bisorio people have a biting sarcasm that they employ to make a point, and Mawiba was about to make a point!

"O, it's a good thing, isn't it, to live in constant fear and terror of the spirits? We would *really* want to return to that, wouldn't we?" George translated and Mawiba continued:

"And it's a *good thing* to worship our dead ancestors and the demons that tormented us, isn't it? We would *really* want to return to that, wouldn't we?" He paused for George to translate, and then he went on;

"O, and murdering each other for revenge; now, that's a really happy way to live isn't it? Especially when we can look forward to being murdered ourselves! Are these the things we want to teach our children? Are these the things we would want to go back to?"

As George translated Mawiba's response, his heart leapt for joy. Yet, the reporter's pencil was strangely quiet! But now, the passionate Bisorio man leaned forward and finished his answer,

"No!" He said emphatically. "The message of Jesus Christ dying for our sins and giving us eternal life...**that** is what we want to give to our children. **That** is what we want the coming generations to believe! We will **never** go back to life without Christ!"

George translated Mawiba's energetic answer to Miss Irewood. She sat for a split second looking blankly at the missionary, and then, she rolled her eyes. Instantly, George understood; this skeptical reporter believed that he had fabricated Mawiba's response!

"Listen," He told her, "I'm just translating word for word what these men have said. I'm not holding up cue cards. They are speaking from their hearts!" She smiled politely and after a few more exchanges, ended the interview. There was not a word written in her notebook!

As the plane, laden with the IBC crew and equipment took off the next day, George, Harriet, Bob and Sue waved goodbye.

"I don't think I want to do that again," sighed Bob.

"That's for sure," replied Sue.

"Do you think they even got an inkling of what the Lord has done in the Bisorios' lives?" Harriett wondered.

"I doubt it," said George. "But *we* know, and most of all," he said with a smile, "the Bisorios know!"

CPSIA information can be obtained at www.ICGtesting.com
Printed in the USA
BVOW05s0257190514

353782BV00003B/112/P